The Formative 5 will not only help teachers deepen their understanding of formative assessment, but it provides them with concrete tools to implement each of the five formative assessment techniques to move students' lea of experiences working with teachers, students, and le their guidance in examples and vignettes that allow re can be implemented in classrooms, making the book v using it with both inservice and preservice teachers wi

—**Robert Q. Berry, III, PhD**
Associate Professor, Curry School of Education, University of Virginia
President-Elect, National Council of Teachers of Mathematics

A great resource for math educators! The easy-to-read format, practical suggestions, and ready-to-use tools give teachers what they need to engage in their own professional learning. I am also excited about the potential impact on teaching and learning for those leaders in our district who take the time to use this resource during their professional learning experiences.

—**Christopher R. Horne, PhD**
Curriculum Specialist for Elementary Science, Frederick County Public Schools, MD

I am so excited about integrating *The Formative Five* into our district's ongoing work with formative assessment. This practitioner friendly resource provides math educators five ready-to-use formative assessment techniques complete with planning tools, examples, and many other useful resources that our district's professional learning communities will use as we continue our work in the teaching and learning of mathematics.

—**Angela Waltrup**
Content Specialist, Elementary Mathematics, Washington County Public Schools, MD

The Formative 5 explains why formative assessment is the lifeblood of all good instruction and then provides practical strategies that teachers can start using tomorrow. Fennell, Kobett, and Wray have given math teachers the best sort of gift—one that serves their students.

—**Eric Westendorf**
Co-Founder and CEO, LearnZillion

The Formative 5 is easy to read and full of specific assessment strategies that can stand alone or be used in concert. The ideas outlined in this book can be used on a daily basis to inform instructional decision making. The grade-level examples of each of the assessment strategies, video examples, and professional learning discussion questions are perfect for use in a preservice teacher education program, in service professional learning environment, or school-based PLC.

—**Kyndall Brown**
Executive Director, California Mathematics Project, UCLA

THE
FORMATIVE 5

To Nita, Brett, Heather, and Stacey for their continuing support and patience! AND, to the elementary mathematics specialists and teacher leaders project's "core group." Your successes, challenges, hopes, dreams, and openness have charted and guided this effort and many others. Thanks for continuing to share, critique, and modify all that we do to make things "work" for teachers and children.

—Francis (Skip) Fennell

To my husband, Tim, and my daughters, Hannah and Jenna Kobett, for their enduring love and support. Also, to our preservice teachers. Your unbridled enthusiasm, commitment to your future students, and passion for learning and teaching inspire us. Thank you for embracing the importance of formative assessment, using the techniques, and providing feedback. Early on, you convinced us that these techniques would not only work, but could transform teaching practices. Our work with you convinces us that the future of education is not just bright, but brilliant.

—Beth McCord Kobett

To my mother, Karen S. Wray, who is the best "teacher" I have ever had. And Julie, Molly, Alanna, Jordan, and Annika—you are truly amazing blessings in my life. We are grateful for the ongoing support from professionals in the Howard County Public School System, around Maryland, and beyond. We hope these techniques inform and impact your daily efforts to ensure that every student achieves mathematical excellence in an inspiring, engaging, and supportive environment.

—Jonathan (Jon) A. Wray

THE
FORMATIVE 5

EVERYDAY ASSESSMENT TECHNIQUES
FOR EVERY MATH CLASSROOM

FRANCIS (SKIP) FENNELL
BETH MCCORD KOBETT
JONATHAN A. WRAY

FOREWORD BY MATT LARSON

A JOINT PUBLICATION

CORWIN
MATHEMATICS

NCTM

NATIONAL COUNCIL OF
TEACHERS OF MATHEMATICS

FOR INFORMATION:

Corwin

A SAGE Company

2455 Teller Road

Thousand Oaks, California 91320

(800) 233-9936

www.corwin.com

SAGE Publications Ltd.

1 Oliver's Yard

55 City Road

London EC1Y 1SP

United Kingdom

SAGE Publications India Pvt. Ltd.

B 1/I 1 Mohan Cooperative Industrial Area

Mathura Road, New Delhi 110 044

India

SAGE Publications Asia-Pacific Pte. Ltd.

3 Church Street

#10–04 Samsung Hub

Singapore 049483

Acquisitions Editor: Erin Null

Editorial Development Manager: Julie Nemer

Editorial Assistant: Nicole Shade

Production Editor: Melanie Birdsall

Copy Editor: Liann Lech

Typesetter: C&M Digitals (P) Ltd.

Proofreader: Theresa Kay

Indexer: Marilyn Augst

Cover and Interior Designer: Rose Storey

Marketing Manager: Margaret O'Connor

Library of Congress Cataloging-in-Publication Data

Names: Fennell, Francis (Skip), | Kobett, Beth McCord, | Wray, Jonathan A.

Title: The formative 5 : everyday assessment techniques for every math classroom / Francis (Skip) Fennell, Beth McCord Kobett, Jonathan A. Wray ; foreword by Matt Larson.

Other titles: Formative five

Description: Thousand Oaks, California : Corwin, [2017] | Includes bibliographical references and index.

Identifiers: LCCN 2016035552 | ISBN 9781506337500 (pbk. : alk. paper)

Subjects: LCSH: Mathematics—Study and teaching—Evaluation.

Classification: LCC QA11 .F46 2017 | DDC 510.71—dc23 LC record available at https://lccn.loc.gov/2016035552

This book is printed on acid-free paper.

Certified Chain of Custody
Promoting Sustainable Forestry
www.sfiprogram.org
SFI-01268

SFI label applies to text stock

17 18 19 20 21 10 9 8 7 6 5 4 3 2 1

CONTENTS

PART III Next Steps   133

CHAPTER 6
IT'S YOUR TURN!

Visit the companion website at
http://resources.corwin.com/Formative5
for downloadable resources, tools, and videos.

Note From the Publisher: The authors have provided video and web content throughout the book that is available to you through QR codes. To read a QR code, you must have a smartphone or tablet with a camera. We recommend that you download a QR code reader app that is made specifically for your phone or tablet brand.

TOOLS FOR YOUR USE

 Blank template versions of the following tools, as well as the Book Study Guide, are available for download at **http://resources.corwin.com/Formative5**

OBSERVATIONS

- Planning: Observations Template
- Small Group: Implementation and Recording Tool for Observations
- Classroom: Observation Checklist
- Classroom: Observation—Student Representations
- Individual Student: Mathematics Strengths Observation Log
- Individual Student: Observation Check-In

INTERVIEWS

- Planning: Interview Tool
- Classroom: Interview Record
- Individual Student: Interview Prompt

SHOW ME

- Small Group: Show Me Record

HINGE QUESTIONS

- Planning: Hinge Question Considerations Tool
- Classroom: Hinge Question Implementation Tool

EXIT TASKS

- Planning: Exit Tasks Tool
- Exit Task Organizer Tool

BOOK STUDY GUIDE

FOREWORD

For the past two decades, both the research and practitioner literature have been replete with the virtues of teachers implementing formative assessment processes in their classrooms. There is good reason for the abundance of advice concerning formative assessment. For example, Popham (2011) has argued on the basis of more than 4,000 research studies that when formative assessment processes are well implemented in the classroom, the speed of student learning is nearly doubled while simultaneously producing large gains in student achievement.

Very few instructional strategies enjoy both the research base and consensus among school-based instructional leaders that formative assessment does with respect to its leverage—if implemented effectively—to improve student learning. Consequently, school leaders have been imploring teachers to implement more formative assessment processes in the classroom. It would be hard to find a teacher today who has not heard some synopsis of the research on formative assessment in a professional development workshop or at a conference. We have reached the point in schools today where nearly every teacher can recite that in their classrooms, they should be engaged in "assessment *for* learning instead of assessment *of* learning." But what does that oft-repeated saying mean in real classrooms? What should teachers be doing? What are the actual *techniques* of classroom formative assessment?

The issue with respect to the implementation of formative assessment processes is the same issue teachers face with respect to many instructional recommendations: teachers are frequently told what they should do, but they are usually not provided clear guidance on how to implement it in their classrooms—theory triumphs over practice. The void between theory and practice is what authors Fennell, Kobett, and Wray, in *The Formative 5*, step into and fill in a highly effective and practitioner-friendly way.

Based on the authors' work with thousands of teachers of mathematics, mathematics specialists, and instructional leaders, Fennell, Kobett, and Wray offer the powerful metaphor of an artist's color palette to describe five formative assessment techniques that they have validated in classrooms with real teachers and students. The metaphor of an artist's palette is critical. While the five techniques stand alone on an artist's palette just as colors do, when blended together they have the potential to create a work of "instructional art" that leads to gains in student learning much greater than the individual techniques.

Each formative assessment technique is effective if implemented on its own, but as the authors recommend, the techniques are most powerful when blended and used together. When blended, the techniques provide a clear picture of student understanding that supports teachers in responding more effectively to student needs and that can be used to guide future instructional decisions. Through all the formative assessment techniques, students are positioned as active and engaged self-assessors in the techniques as they monitor and guide their own learning.

For each of the five techniques, the authors provide background and cite the literature supporting the technique so that you can rest assured the technique has its foundation in the research on formative assessment. The authors go on to provide guidance for how you can plan to implement the technique in your classroom through a set of planning questions. Most authors would stop here. But Fennell, Kobett, and Wray go well beyond this level of guidance by providing various grade-level examples that can be used to visualize the techniques in action in the classroom, as well as multiple tools unique to each technique that you can use to plan, implement, and reflect on the technique's effectiveness in your classroom.

At the end of each chapter, the authors provide discussion questions to support you and your colleagues as you work in your professional learning communities to continually improve your formative assessment, lesson planning, and instructional effectiveness. The final chapter offers responses to frequently asked questions the authors have encountered as they worked with teachers implementing the Formative 5 techniques. These questions and responses bring the authors into your classroom to support you as you work to make the Formative 5 techniques part of your daily instructional practice.

If the authors offered nothing more than the specific guidance and tools for the Formative 5 assessment techniques, they would make a significant contribution to improving your practice and your students' learning. But the real strength of this book lies in how the authors integrate instructional planning, teaching, and assessment. One of the challenges in American education is that, as classroom teachers, we all too often fail to collaborate with our colleagues to plan instruction. We might cooperate and pace out our instruction together, but we don't truly collaborate with our colleagues to plan and reflect on the instructional techniques we use in the classroom.

Fennell, Kobett, and Wray make a strong case that when instruction is optimal, the concepts of planning, instruction, and formative assessment become virtually indistinguishable—they all become components of one seamless process delivering powerful instruction that positively impacts student learning. In *The Formative 5,* Fennell, Kobett, and Wray provide a study guide with tools you can leverage as part of your professional learning team to guide your collaborative reading of the book, gain new insights, and discuss implementation with members of your collaborative learning team. The authors don't just argue you should collaborate with your colleagues—they give you the tools with which to authentically collaborate and improve your practice!

This book is a gem. Fennell, Kobett, and Wray don't just provide advice on what to do; they provide you the tools you need to implement specific formative assessment techniques in *your* classroom. I encourage you to read it with your colleagues and discuss the questions, collaborate around the tools to plan instruction, and implement the Formative 5 techniques in your classroom. When you do this, you will see that planning, instruction, and assessment are all part of a larger "teaching palette" that, when effectively blended, come together to significantly and positively impact student learning. Enjoy!

—Matt Larson, PhD
National Council of Teachers of
Mathematics President (2016–2018)

ABOUT THE AUTHORS

Francis (Skip) Fennell, PhD, is emeritus as the L. Stanley Bowlsbey Professor of Education and Graduate and Professional Studies at McDaniel College in Maryland, where he directs the Elementary Mathematics Specialists and Teacher Leaders Project. He is a former classroom teacher, principal, and supervisor of instruction, and past president of the Association of Mathematics Teacher Educators (AMTE), the Research Council for Mathematics Learning (RCML), and the National Council of Teachers of Mathematics (NCTM). He is a recipient of the Mathematics Educator of the Year Award from the Maryland Council of Teachers of Mathematics (MCTM), the Glenn Gilbert National Leadership Award from the National Council of Supervisors of Mathematics (NCSM), the Excellence in Leadership and Service in Mathematics Teacher Education Award from the Association of Mathematics Teacher Educators (AMTE), and the Lifetime Achievement Award from the National Council of Teachers of Mathematics (NCTM).

Beth McCord Kobett, EdD, is an assistant professor in the School of Education at Stevenson University, where she works with preservice teachers and leads professional learning efforts in mathematics education both regionally and nationally. She is also the lead consultant for the Elementary Mathematics Specialists and Teacher Leaders Project. She is a former classroom teacher, elementary mathematics specialist, adjunct professor, and university supervisor. She is the current president of the Association of Maryland Mathematics Teacher Educators (AMMTE) and chair of the Professional Development Services Committee of the National Council of Teachers of Mathematics (NCTM). Dr. Kobett is a recipient of the Mathematics Educator of the Year Award from the Maryland Council of Teachers of Mathematics (MCTM). She also received Stevenson University's Excellence in Teaching Award as both an adjunct and full-time member of the Stevenson faculty.

Jonathan A. Wray is the Instructional Facilitator for Secondary Mathematics in the Howard County Public School System. He is also the Project Manager of the Elementary Mathematics Specialists and Teacher Leaders Project. He recently completed a term as an elected member of the National Council of Teachers of Mathematics' (NCTM) Board of Directors. He is a former elementary classroom teacher, mathematics resource teacher, and past president of both the Association of Maryland Mathematics Teacher Educators (AMMTE) and the Maryland Council of Teachers of Mathematics (MCTM). Mr. Wray is a recipient of the MCTM Outstanding Teacher Mentor Award, and was selected as his district's Outstanding Technology Leader in Education by the Maryland Society for Educational Technology.

> **❝** I never really thought much about assessment other than the tests I would create and use or the end-of-year standardized required tests we used. **❞**

— FIFTH-GRADE TEACHER

> **❝** Formative assessment is so talked about, but it seems mysterious to me. **❞**

— KINDERGARTEN TEACHER

> **❝** I have enough trouble with thinking about and planning for my teaching, how does my principal expect me to involve assessment too—beyond our unit and end-of-year required tests? **❞**

— SEVENTH-GRADE TEACHER

PREFACE

The Elementary Mathematics Specialists and Teacher Leaders Project (http://www.mathspecialists.org) endeavors to both identify and address challenges and concerns expressed by the mathematics specialists/instructional leaders and classroom teachers with whom we work, both regionally and nationally. One of those challenges that has been regularly expressed is related to assessment. What we were hearing were comments, like those above, that appeared to be clearly seeking to understand the role of assessment generally, but, in particular, how it could and should impact classroom instruction.

Our efforts for the past few years have been dedicated to addressing the important role of formative assessment and its everyday connection to planning and instruction. Our analysis revealed, as others have noted, that we actually do know a lot about formative assessment, and one of the things we know is that it can and does make a difference. We also found that when we asked teachers and mathematics specialists/leaders about formative assessment, we received many different responses and definitions. Additionally, far too many of our respondents indicated that assessment, to them, was a "special moment" often defined by others, as in end-of-year external assessments, rather than regularly connected to their planning and teaching. Finally, we recognized an overload of publications, actual published formative assessments, worksheets, and services advertised as the formative assessment "fix" for the classroom or school level.

This book has been guided by the research of Wiliam and Thompson (2007) and focuses on the importance of minute-by-minute and day-by-day or short-cycle formative assessment and particular strategies for effective formative assessment. It's all about assessment to inform teaching and learning—every day. *The Formative 5* represents a distillation and validation of classroom-based formative assessment techniques that teachers can use on a regular basis. We think of the Formative 5 techniques as a palette of five "colors" that teachers can use, sometimes mixing the colors to find the best way to formatively assess as well as guide planning, teaching, and learning every day.

The book's chapters include an introductory chapter that discusses issue and opportunities related to assessment in general, and formative assessment in particular, and also prepares readers for the following specific chapters dedicated to each of the Formative 5 assessment techniques: Observations (Chapter 1), Interviews (Chapter 2), Show Me (Chapter 3), Hinge Questions (Chapter 4), and Exit Tasks (Chapter 5). The Formative 5 chapters each include suggestions for use of that particular technique in the classroom as well as accompanying tools that can be used to guide planning and teaching and record student responses. You will find blank versions of the tools that you may download and adapt for your own use at the book's companion website, **http://resources.corwin.com/ Formative5.** In Chapters 2 and 3, you'll also find QR codes that link to audio and video samples we have captured of students engaged in interviews and Show Me moments so that you can see their work and hear their thinking. These are meant to demonstrate what these techniques look and sound like as captured in the classroom. Chapter 6, the book's final chapter, summarizes and addresses frequently asked questions related to the previous chapters and provides comments designed to encourage and support YOUR implementation of the Formative 5. Finally, the book's appendix can be used to guide a book study that directs reading and related discussion of each of the Formative 5 techniques as well as their integration within an everyday classroom implementation plan for formative assessment.

ACKNOWLEDGMENTS

While the three of us are engaged in a myriad of activities, research projects, service opportunities, and a steady stream of publications related to mathematics education, we pride ourselves in never having left our roots—the classroom and the everyday needs of classroom teachers. We truly respect and formally acknowledge how their needs, efforts, and challenges have influenced our work, and the development, vetting, and publication of *The Formative 5* in particular.

We would also like to acknowledge and thank the Brookhill Institute of Mathematics, especially Kathy Stumpf, President, for recognizing the potential of and supporting the Elementary Mathematics Specialists and Teacher Leaders (ems&tl) Project. Our work with mathematics specialists and mathematics leaders has provided us with the wings to create, question, and respond to issues of importance to mathematics education, including the development of the Formative 5.

Finally, a special acknowledgment to Corwin, and Erin Null, Acquisitions Editor; Melanie Birdsall, Senior Project Editor; and Liann Lech, Copy Editor, with a particular heartfelt thanks to Erin for recognizing the potential of the Formative 5 and relentlessly encouraging, supporting, and prodding the development of this book.

Publisher's Acknowledgments

Corwin gratefully acknowledges the contributions of the following reviewers:

Natalie Crist
Elementary Mathematics Specialist
Baltimore County Public Schools
Towson, MD

Russell Gersten
Executive Director of Educational Research Institute
Instructional Research Group
Los Alamitos, CA

PART I

GETTING STARTED

"When I first heard about assessment, I just figured they were talking about our end-of-year state-required tests."

—FIFTH-GRADE TEACHER

"Why didn't I learn about formative assessment in my teacher prep program?"

—FIRST-YEAR TEACHER

"I just figured I could search online and buy whatever formative assessment I needed for math."

—MIDDLE SCHOOL TEACHER

WHY FORMATIVE ASSESSMENT?

ISSUES AND OPPORTUNITIES

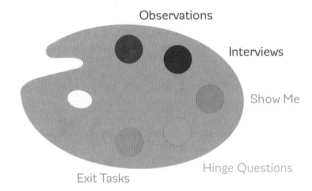

Assessment Literacy: What Is It? Why Is This Important?

Assessment of student learning is the responsibility of every school district, every school, and every teacher. In a report prepared for the Council for the Accreditation of Educator Preparation, Kahl, Hofman, and Bryant (2012) found that in many preservice teacher education programs, attention to assessment literacy was incomplete, rendering many, if not most, beginning teachers unprepared for the actual use and interpretation of assessments. Major tenets of assessment literacy include being able to create, select, and effectively use classroom assessments and being able to select and effectively interpret and use results from external summative assessments.

Included among the understandings and skills that encompass assessment literacy are teacher expectations related to the identification, selection, or creation of assessments designed for monitoring student growth and the diagnosis of specific student needs, which is essentially what this book is all about—formative assessment. Important issues related to analyzing and evaluating the evidence generated by summative assessment is really important too, but that's perhaps another book for another time. Our focus will be on assessment literacy as it relates, every day, to the classroom—YOUR classroom. Consider this chapter as the beginning of a journey that will start with an overview of particular issues and challenges related to assessment and then move to address, more directly, the classroom-based formative assessment techniques that are the focus of this book, and that you will use every day.

Formative/Summative: It's All Testing, Right?

> ❝ I actually never knew that my end-of-year and end-of-marking period benchmark tests in mathematics were summative assessments. Thinking about how I can use both formative and summative assessments has been an eye-opening experience to me, AND I'm in my fifth year of teaching! ❞
>
> —FOURTH-GRADE TEACHER

Assessment at the PreK–12 level has long been an assumed responsibility of the classroom teacher. You assess to compare students, guide and influence instruction, and evaluate (e.g., evaluating a curricular program or instructional technique). Think about each of these purposes. When are you assessing to compare? To influence instruction? To evaluate? And, importantly, how much instructional time are you and your school district devoting to assessment? How are you using the assessment results—both assessments that you create and use and those external summative assessments that you are responsible for administering (e.g., school district, state, or other mandated assessments)? Some argue, perhaps appropriately, that external summative tests are taking way too much time away from teaching and learning. For example, in *Testing More, Teaching Less* (Nelson, 2013), it was revealed that in one school district studied, students spent up to fifty-five hours per year taking tests. (That's about two full weeks of the school year.) One of the school districts studied had twelve different district and external summative assessments that accounted for forty-seven separate administrations of these assessments over the course of one instructional year.

As a classroom teacher, your day-to-day involvement with assessment should be in the consideration and use of classroom-based formative assessments, while acknowledging the role and potential of summative assessment. Let's start this by considering, and even defining, both formative and summative assessment.

Formative assessment has been discussed and seemingly defined and redefined for more than fifty years. Scriven (1967) and Bloom (1969) were early advocates of the power of formative evaluation to improve instruction. Based on their review of hundreds of studies, of which 250 were directly relevant to formative assessment, Black and Wiliam (1998) defined formative assessment "as encompassing all those activities undertaken by teachers and/or by their students, which provide information to be used as feedback to modify the teaching and learning activities in which they are engaged" (p. 7). Formative assessment includes all activities that provide information to be used as feedback to modify teaching and learning. Our focus is on the everyday use of classroom-based formative assessments to monitor, probe, and provide feedback designed to impact planning and teaching.

Summative assessments are typically used to assess student learning at the end of an experience. This could be a unit assessment, school district assessment, or the more high-stakes and high-profile end-of-year state assessments. Many summative assessments are externally created, that is, prepared by others. Summative assessments are typically used to compare. Such comparisons could be student-to-student or class-to-class, or the extent to which results address predetermined standards or expectations. Summative assessments are regularly used to identify score-based differences among individual students or among groups of students. These comparisons often lead to classifications of student scores on a student-by-student basis or on a group-by-group basis, using norms or defined levels of performance (e.g., advanced, proficient, developing, not yet met). Summative assessment results or even performance on particular items can be used formatively when grade-level teams analyze results and use them to guide instructional goals and classroom activities. The Every Student Succeeds Act, signed by President Barack Obama in December 2015, requires that all students complete a state-determined summative assessment in Grades 3–8 and once at the high school level. However, states now have flexibility in how and when they administer the tests (e.g., a single annual assessment can be broken down into a series of smaller tests). There's also an emphasis on finding different kinds of summative tests that more accurately measure what students are learning. To summarize the differences, many characterize summative assessments as assessments *of* learning and formative assessments as assessments *for* learning.

This book addresses a specific need with regard to formative assessment, which is to identify and provide specific suggestions on how to use particular classroom-based formative assessment techniques on a regular—daily—basis. Our book is not about

> Formative assessment includes all activities that provide information to be used as feedback to modify teaching and learning.

> Summative assessments are typically used to assess student learning at the end of an experience. This could be a unit assessment, school district assessment, or the more high-stakes and high-profile end-of-year state assessments.

high-stakes summative assessments and the perceived, by many, overuse of such assessments. What we offer is designed to connect planning, teaching, and assessment in YOUR classroom every day.

Formative Assessment: Assessing to In*form*

    I never 'got' formative assessment. It just seemed to be like try this and try that. So many things to consider. Then I had this professor and he used the painter's palette analogy. Small number of paints to choose from, which could be mixed and applied using various techniques and used daily. Bingo. Got it. And now I use these classroom-based formative assessment techniques every day.

—MATH SPECIALIST/INSTRUCTIONAL LEADER

Black and Wiliam (2009) noted that assessment becomes formative "to the extent that evidence about student achievement is elicited, interpreted, and used by teachers, learners, or their peers, to make decisions about the next steps in instruction" (p. 9). As stated previously, we know that formative assessment has been defined, redefined, researched, and discussed for decades. *Education Week* ("Understanding formative assessment," 2015) noted that formative assessment is both widely used and poorly understood! Some argue that the phrase *formative assessment* is open to too many interpretations. Stiggins (2005) and others actually prefer the phrase *assessment for learning*. Our position is that formative assessment is an integral component of what you do every day—planning and teaching—and that it involves a carefully defined and vetted set of assessment techniques specifically designed to in*form* instruction.

As a teacher, you are involved every single day in planning and teaching and then repeating that process. Assessment is integral to both planning and teaching. Linda Darling-Hammond (1994) noted that "in order for assessment to support student learning, it must include teachers in all stages of the process and be embedded in curriculum and teaching activities" (p. 25).

Directly connecting assessment to planning and teaching within each lesson provides both the foundation and consistency in approach to truly influence teaching and learning. So, for instance, as you plan, consider not only mathematics content (e.g., place value) but also how the Standards for Mathematical Practice (National Governors Association Center for Best Practices and

Directly connecting assessment to planning and teaching within each lesson can truly influence teaching and learning.

Council of Chief State School Officers [NGA Center & CCSSO], 2010) will be integrally involved within a lesson. Linking assessment to planning in*forms* both teaching and learning (*form* within in*form* is italicized to bring attention to the central role of classroom-based formative assessment as it in*forms* teaching and learning).

Wiliam and Thompson (2007) suggest that the effective use of assessment for learning consists of five key strategies:

1. **Clarifying and sharing learning intentions and criteria for success with learners:**

> Paige cut three pieces of rope, and each piece was $1\frac{1}{2}$ meters long. She placed the rope pieces end-to-end. She thought she had > 5 meters of rope. Was she right? Can you show me how you decided if Paige was right or wrong?

The focus here is on your unpacking of the intended learning goals of a lesson and then determining the mathematical tasks and related activities that will lead to the expected learning. The example of the problem involving Paige above provides a beginning task in multiplying whole numbers and fractions. The Show Me response requested (this formative assessment technique is the focus of Chapter 3) should demonstrate a level of understanding related to the mathematical intent of the lesson.

2. **Engineering effective classroom discussions, questions, and learning tasks that elicit evidence of students' learning:**

> Using a rectangular region, show me three ways to represent fractions equivalent to $\frac{1}{4}$.

> If we doubled the length of each side of a square, what happens to the area of the square?

This assessment strategy considers how you will develop classroom activities that not only engage students in doing mathematics, but provide evidence of student progress toward intended mathematics goals. The emphasis here is on finding the time to plan for each lesson with consideration for what and how you will assess student progress. Think about what you would assess for each of the examples above. Careful planning—including attention to questioning, particularly the lesson's hinge question (more on that later)—and engineering the discussion of learning tasks address assessment *for* learning rather than *of* learning.

3. Providing feedback that moves learners forward:

> Great job! All five answers are correct.

> You solved the first three correctly. Look at problems 4 and 5 and see if you can find your error, and then show me how you would do these problems differently.

You provide feedback to your students every day. However, the most important thing about feedback is what students do with it. If your feedback prompted students to try a different solution strategy and they do so, then the feedback was helpful. Perhaps your feedback just affirms a student's response like the first example above. Whether or not specific feedback to your students "works" is really something that you can control. The more you observe your students as they engage in learning mathematics, the more you will get to know them and provide personalized feedback when they need it. In the second boxed example above, you may want to linger with the student so that the Show Me response can be quickly reviewed and additional feedback provided as needed.

4. Activating students as owners of their own learning:

> I like that pattern. Can you provide the next three numbers in the pattern and, as you do that, tell me why you have included them?

> Show me how you know that multiples are different from factors.

Using formative assessment to monitor teaching and learning is not a one-way, teacher-to-student trip. The intent is to engage students in learning mathematics, which includes students taking an active role as they monitor and guide their own learning. One intent of formative assessment is to help students, all students, take an active role in and ownership of their learning. Such inclusive ownership and self-assessment opportunities will impact the pace of particular lessons and also have you consider particular formative assessment techniques. Your use of observation, interviews, Show Me, hinge questions, and exit tasks, the classroom-based formative assessment techniques presented in this book, will include the consideration of students as respondents, active learners, and fully engaged self-assessors.

One intent of formative assessment is help students, all students, take an active role in and ownership of their learning.

5. **Activating students as instructional resources for one another:**

> **Teacher:** Work that problem out with your partner and be prepared to share the solution with the class.
>
> **Cam:** When I looked at how Quinn solved the problem, I really liked what he did. Next time I might try thinking about percent his way—rather than finding what you pay if it's 25 percent off, which is a two-step problem, thinking about the problem as 75 percent on (just subtracting 25 percent off mentally) turns it into just a "one-stepper." I like that.

Paired learning and small group learning activities are instructional strategies you have most likely used throughout your teaching career. The formative assessment potential of peer review is in developing responsible collaboration among students. The result is that students learn from each other. Perhaps more importantly, students are often more willing to accept feedback from a peer than an authority figure (e.g., teacher, parent . . .) even when such student-to-student feedback is generally concisely presented and often very direct (e.g., "Why would you do it that way?" "No way that answer is even close.").

What we know about formative assessment is that student achievement can be improved when teachers regularly use it both within and between lessons. Our approach to classroom-based formative assessment has been to focus on what Wiliam and Thompson (2007) have defined as short-cycle formative assessment—day by day and minute by minute. Our experience has been that such assessment is integral to and within every lesson, with the potential to impact students between lessons as well. While we recognize the importance of all of the key strategies discussed above, our approach particularly emphasizes and promotes the following two strategies:

> *Engineering effective classroom discussions, questions, and learning tasks that elicit evidence of students' learning*
>
> *Providing feedback that moves learners forward*

The everyday use and related student responses and feedback to the formative assessment techniques presented here are intended to guide and in*form* your everyday planning and instruction.

Classroom-Based Formative Assessment: Why Is This Important? You Do Have the Time to Do This!

❝ It took me years to realize that assessment, particularly what I do in the area of classroom assessment, isn't some stand-alone 'other thing' I am supposed to be doing as required by my school's supervisor. Hello, why didn't anyone tell me?! ❞

—FOURTH-GRADE TEACHER

❝ Formative assessment? I just thought it was something I was required to do. ❞

—KINDERGARTEN TEACHER

When you create, select, administer, and then evaluate the results of *any* assessment, formative or summative, you estimate the value of the responses and use that to determine what students know. Important stuff. By November of any given instructional year, you have a sense of what each student in your mathematics classroom knows and is able to do. But the reality is, much of what you do assessment-wise is, or should be, directly related to what you teach—every single day. That's how we envision formative assessment. As noted earlier, the focus of this book is classroom-based formative assessment—the use of particular assessment techniques that you can and should use every day to not only validate and build on prior assessments, but also guide your planning and teaching. Why? Consider NCTM's *Principles to Actions* (2014): "An excellent mathematics program ensures that assessment is an integral part of instruction, provides evidence of proficiency with important mathematics content and practices, includes a variety of strategies and data sources, and informs feedback to students, instructional decisions and program improvement" (p. 89). The point here is that assessment must be an everyday component of what you do as you plan and teach. Assessing while you teach—it's what you do. You plan and teach, and as you teach a lesson, any lesson, you can—and should—use particular assessment techniques to monitor student progress within the lesson, as well as the lesson itself.

In our early work with formative assessment, we recognized—and mathematics specialists and teachers told us—that there were so many suggestions and ideas related to formative assessment that

Assessing while you teach—it's what you do.

understanding and using them was never well understood. And, in some cases, all of the hype regarding formative assessment put the specialists and teachers on overload. This got our attention. We have spent time distilling and validating, through classroom use, a small set of classroom-based formative assessment techniques that teachers have used successfully on a regular basis. We like to think of these classroom-based formative assessment techniques metaphorically as a palette of five "colors" that you can use as you paint your own classroom canvas, sometimes mixing the colors to find the best way to formatively assess and guide teaching and learning on a daily basis. Later in this chapter, and much more specifically and in depth in the chapters that follow, we will discuss the five techniques, which we call the Formative 5—observations, interviews, Show Me, hinge questions, and exit tasks.

Let's think about formative assessment as it links to your own daily and even long-term planning for instruction. As you plan, you consider the mathematical focus of the lesson. An important prerequisite to such planning is your own understanding of the mathematical content and pedagogical knowledge related to your grade level and beyond. We fully recognize that it takes time for you to understand the learning trajectories of the mathematics content topics for which you are responsible, as well as how to interpret and address them in your classroom. For example, for a lesson at the fourth-grade level related to equivalent fractions, some of your students may be able to move quickly into extensions involving comparing and ordering fractions, while others may have difficulty representing common equivalent fractions. As you know, such a range within a single mathematics topic is not uncommon. However, your ability to plan based on knowledge of your students and their mathematical needs is important. This certainly includes particular tasks you may select and design to match your lesson's mathematical focus, and, importantly, how you will assess student performance and the overall impact and effectiveness of your lesson. In short, as you plan, you should anticipate what you expect your students to accomplish. So, yes, what and how you will assess is part of both planning and teaching. Your teaching will reflect the formative assessment techniques you had planned to use to monitor student progress and the lesson's overall effectiveness. The following questions may help guide your planning and teaching as related to your use of formative assessment:

- What tasks and questions will be used to engage students in the lesson?

- How will learning trajectories of the mathematics content focus of the lesson be considered to ensure the developmental appropriateness and student prerequisite background for this lesson?

- How will you communicate student learning expectations for this lesson?
- When and how will students receive feedback for their contributions during the lesson?
- What responsibilities do your students have for assessing their learning in this lesson?
- How will formative assessment be used to monitor student progress in this lesson?
- Will students be assessed individually, in groups, or both individually and within a group?
- How will formative assessment be used to determine the effectiveness of the lesson?

Now let's consider the specific classroom-based formative assessment techniques that you can use in your classroom.

Formative Assessment in YOUR Classroom: The Classroom Is *Your* Canvas!

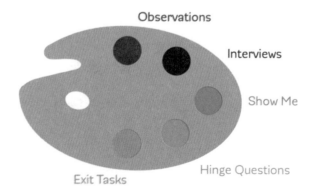

> I actually never thought much about using formative assessment every day and had no idea how it connected with my planning and teaching. So glad we decided to use observation, interviews, Show Me, hinge questions, and exit tasks regularly. I get it now, and my kids have actually come to expect the hinge question and exit tasks.
>
> —THIRD-GRADE TEACHER

As noted earlier, this book presents five classroom-based formative assessment techniques, the Formative 5, which you can use every day. Using the metaphor of an artist's palette of five colors, the assessment techniques can be ordered and mixed based on your planning and instructional needs. The chapters that follow will present, discuss, and provide tools for using the Formative 5 techniques—observations, interviews, Show Me, hinge questions, and exit tasks—in your classroom. This palette of formative assessment techniques has been gleaned from the seemingly endless suggestions provided for classroom consideration and use and have been carefully defined and tested in classrooms. A brief summary of each of the Formative 5 techniques is provided below.

> The palette of formative assessment techniques can be ordered and mixed based on your planning and instructional needs.

Observations. You observe your students every day—throughout the day. While this technique may be the most informal classroom-based formative assessment, its use is of particular importance to you as you monitor a lesson. As you use observation as a classroom-based formative assessment technique, the following questions, which will be discussed in depth in Chapter 1, will be helpful as you plan for the use of this technique.

1. What would you hope to observe your students doing in this mathematics lesson?

2. How would you know "it" if you saw it?

3. Are there particular challenges or difficulties you may observe (conceptual or procedural)?

4. What misconceptions might you observe?

5. How might you record/note what you observe?

A major intent of the observations chapter (Chapter 1) is to provide the background and support tools that should assist you in using observation as a formative assessment technique to guide and in*form* your planning and teaching and monitor student progress.

Interviews. An interview extends an observation. These two techniques are almost always connected. The interview provides the obvious follow-up to an observation a teacher might make when implementing a lesson. An interview also allows the teacher to spend a few valuable minutes digging deeper with an individual student or perhaps a small group of students. The goal of the interview is to get a glimpse of what a student is thinking. A full discussion of the interview technique, including helpful interview tools, is provided in Chapter 2. The questions below, also presented in Chapter 2, should help guide your use of the interview technique.

1. What would make you decide to work with a student one-on-one or with a small group of students?

2. What interview questions might you ask? How might the questions be different for particular students?

3. What will you anticipate from students response-wise? (Consider both understandings *and* possible misconceptions.)

4. What follow-up interview questions might you ask?

The Interviews chapter will provide you with the background and tools appropriate to conduct, analyze, and use interviews to both monitor student progress and guide your planning and teaching.

Show Me. Show Me is a performance-based response by a student and, like the interview, extends an observation. Show Me occurs when a student, pair of students, small group, or perhaps the entire class might be asked to show how something works, how a problem was solved, how a particular manipulative material or related representation was used, and so on. Teachers and mathematics leaders who have used the Show Me technique have noted that it validated information gathered from an observation and/or interview and often provided the first step in redirecting student responses. The following questions have proven to be helpful when anticipating use of the Show Me technique.

1. How is your Show Me different from an observation and interview?

2. What will you use as a prompt for a Show Me request for this lesson?

3. What might you want a student or students to show and say as they describe their Show Me response?

Chapter 3, the Show Me chapter, provides a full discussion and includes a variety of related tools useful for presenting and using the Show Me technique. The observation-interview-Show Me techniques are all quite connected. You will use each of them every day, with the observation typically, but not always, helping to define the specifics of the interview and Show Me opportunities.

Hinge Question. The hinge question (Wiliam, 2011) provides a check for understanding/proficiency at a "hinge point" in a lesson. The hinge question is a question that you plan for and use to elicit responses indicating your next step planning-wise and instructionally, with particular implications for the next day's lesson. Responses to the hinge question directly in*form* both planning and instruction.

Creating the hinge question is an important part of the planning of the day's lesson. Our experience has been that teachers need to take the time to create a question that truly assesses the major focus of the day's lesson. We often consider the hinge question as the lesson's "deal-breaker" since responses help you to determine your next steps instructionally. We have also found it helpful to actually try out hinge questions with colleagues within a grade-level professional learning community. Such trial opportunities also provide teachers with occasions to consider varied hinge question formats. Most importantly, your ability to engineer the use of the hinge question is critical. Considering how you will engage students, assess responses, provide feedback, and decide instructional next steps attests to both the value and importance of the hinge question. Suggestions for the use and types of hinge questions are presented in Chapter 4. This will be a particularly important chapter for you.

Exit Tasks. The National Council of Teachers of Mathematics' *Principles to Actions* (NCTM, 2014) emphasizes the importance of using tasks to elicit student learning and then using the resulting analysis to inform instruction. We consider exit tasks as end-of-lesson formative assessments. We deliberately define such assessments as exit tasks given our experience with the seemingly increasingly popular use of exit tickets or exit slips. The exit task is designed to provide a capstone problem/task that captures the major focus of the mathematics lesson for that day or perhaps the past several days. The use of such problem-based tasks is quite different from the exit tickets or exit slips we have reviewed that tend to address particular mathematical procedures or provide opportunities for students to rate their level of understanding on the mathematics topic of the day. The exit task is actually a product, providing actual work samples for you to review and use for future planning. Like the hinge question, planning time will be needed to develop the exit task, and such task development is enhanced when school or grade-level teacher learning communities work together in their creation, use, and revision. Questions to consider in exit task development include, but are not limited to, the following:

1. Does the exit task capture the mathematics content expectations of your lesson?

2. Given the grade level, classroom norms, and prior experience working with challenging mathematical tasks, will this exit task engage your students?

3. Should the exit task be completed by individual students, student pairs, or small groups?

4. When will you be able to review exit task responses and use the responses to guide your planning as well as provide feedback to your students?

The exit task chapter (Chapter 5) includes multiple examples of exit tasks and tools guiding their use. Given the performance and product nature of the exit task, it is not likely that you would use the exit task every day. Our experience has been that teachers use exit tasks two to three days per week and that the student responses guide not only daily but longer term planning.

Summing Up

Consider the title of this section: Why Formative Assessment? Issues and Opportunities. Even without thinking about it, you assess student progress all day long, every day. You observe, you talk to your students about what they are learning, you ask students to show you what they are doing, you ask questions, and so much more. The chapter started by discussing the importance of assessment literacy, and we recognize that such understanding is the foundation to truly recognizing the importance of both formative and summative assessment and how, in particular, formative assessment can and must guide and monitor your teaching every single day. That's what this chapter and the following chapters are all about—understanding the opportunities related to classroom-based formative assessment and considering how you can make a difference as you connect your planning and teaching to particular classroom-based formative assessment techniques—the Formative 5. This palette of formative assessment techniques— observations, interviews, Show Me, hinge questions, and exit tasks—was presented briefly in this chapter and will be thoroughly discussed and analyzed, with lots of tools supporting its use, in subsequent chapters. The Formative 5 techniques represent our response to addressing issues and opportunities related to formative assessment. Let's get started.

Notes

_____

_____

_____

_____

_____

_____

_____

_____

_____

_____

_____

_____

_____

_____

_____

_____

_____

_____

_____

_____

_____

_____

_____

_____

_____

_____

_____

_____

_____

_____

Professional Learning Discussion Questions

Read and discuss the following questions with your grade-level teaching team or with teams across multiple grade levels. Take notes here or use the tools in the Book Study Guide to record your thoughts.

How does (or perhaps should) the use of formative assessment influence your instructional planning?

How much time do you spend each day as you assess student progress in mathematics?

How much time do you spend each month *and* during the entire school year assessing your students? Make sure to include the summative assessments you administer as well as the formative assessments you may provide.

In your own words, describe the differences between formative and summative assessments.

What formative assessment techniques are you currently using?

What concerns you the most about your use of formative assessment every day?

What concerns you the most about the imbalance, particularly as emphasized in reporting to parents and in the media, between formative and summative assessment?

How do you provide feedback to your students with regard to the assessments that you use?

Is there a difference in how assessment feedback is provided based on the developmental level of students? Does the mathematics content being assessed impact how you provide feedback on such assessments?

PART II

THE FORMATIVE 5

> " How is observation assessment? Of course I observe my students—all day long every day! I just never considered the assessment potential of my observations! "

—FIRST-GRADE TEACHER

> " I actually know more about my students because I am always watching them work and also seeing how they interact—with the mathematics they are learning and with each other. For me, observation is my everyday formative assessment lifeline! "

—FOURTH-GRADE TEACHER

CHAPTER 1

OBSERVATIONS

Observations: Background and Basics

As you consider classroom-based formative assessments, the observation is your "first stop" in the everyday application of the Formative 5. By **observation**, we mean directly observing student and class progress on particular mathematics activities. Observing is what you do every day, all day long. You watch, you notice, but the intent here is to consider how you will use observations, every day, as a formative assessment technique that is closely aligned to your planning and teaching. In our development and use of this book's palette of formative assessment techniques, we have found that the observation, while perhaps the most informal and readily used of the five formative assessment techniques presented (Chapters 1–5), is both taken for granted and, at least to an extent, the least understood of the five techniques.

A quick look at research involving the use of observation includes decades of support for its use. Note that years ago, Freudenthal (1973) indicated that "we know it is more informative to observe a student during a mathematical activity than to grade his papers" (p. 84). More recently, observation-like research related to noticing (Jacobs, Lamb, & Philipp, 2010) has documented how teachers notice children's mathematical thinking. In other words, what has been documented supports the seemingly obvious importance of paying attention to what you see in the classroom and suggests that you spend time anticipating what you might notice or observe, which is what this chapter is all about. **Professional noticing** is "a set of interrelated skills which include (a) attending to children's strategies, (b) interpreting children's understandings, and (c) deciding how to respond on the basis of children's understandings" (Jacobs et al., 2010, p. 172).

Planning for Observations

Let's begin to think about your own planning and the use of observation as a formative assessment technique. The first step in your daily planning, of course, is determining the mathematical focus of a lesson and how your students will be engaged in the mathematics they are learning. Along with such mathematical and instructional intentions should be the consideration of how you will

> **Observation** is directly observing student and class progress on particular mathematics activities.

> **Professional noticing** is "a set of interrelated skills which include (a) attending to children's strategies, (b) interpreting children's understandings, and (c) deciding how to respond on the basis of children's understandings" (Jacobs et al., 2010, p. 172).

use observation. The following questions should help you as you anticipate how you will connect observation to the planning process.

- What will you look for as you observe your students engaging in mathematics?
- How will you use what you observe to monitor the pace and sequence of the day's lesson?
- What can you take away from what you have observed to help in planning for the next day?
- How might you provide feedback to your students, assess what you observe, and record progress?

These anticipatory questions should help you in truly connecting planning to this classroom-based formative assessment technique. Eric's narrative below is fairly typical of early connections with planning and the use of assessment.

> I've been teaching for eight years, and I never thought much about formative assessment. It seemed vague—so many ideas about what it was and how I should be using it—but I was never really plugged into why and the actual specifics of how to use it. So, over the last year or so as we have been using what we call the 'Formative 5,' when I sit down after school or at night and actually plan my lesson, I have gotten to the point where I anticipate what I might observe in my lesson and think hard about what it might look like. Then, pretty important here, I think about what I might do with what I observe—whether that's moving to another of the Formative 5 or considering feedback with my students or thinking about what I have just observed and how it will impact my planning for the next day. This has all become pretty routine now, but I admit that I could have always done this, I just never realized the power and importance of observing.

Eric's growth in understanding the value of observation and using this technique helped in the development of the guiding questions for daily use of observation, and its connection to your planning and teaching (see Figure 1.1).

The questions in Figure 1.1 are intended to guide you as you consider whether and how you will use observations to monitor instruction and student learning. The following examples, at various grade levels, provide actual considerations for use of the guiding

Figure 1.1 • Planning for Observations

1. What would you expect to observe?

- As you plan a lesson, anticipate what you would expect students to be doing as they engage in the mathematics focus of the day's lesson.

2. How would you know "it" if you saw it?

- As you plan and then think about teaching a lesson, how would you know if what you expected to observe actually occurred?
- This consideration sharpens the first question and extends it from what you anticipate or expect to the actual reality of considering responses—and that's assessment.

3. What mathematical challenges or misconceptions might you observe?

- As you get ready to finalize how and what you will observe within a lesson, it just makes sense to reflect on your experience in teaching mathematics.
- What are the "bumps" in your lesson that you may want to especially look for or observe?
- Are such "bumps" related to conceptual understandings, procedures, the use of representations, use of specific mathematics vocabulary, being able to write a response to a problem's solution, or something else?

4. How might you record and provide feedback of what you observed?

- What tools would you use and how frequently would you use them to more formally monitor what you observe?
- In particular, see the Tools for Using Observations in the Classroom section of this chapter for examples of individual student, small group, and classroom observation tools.
- As you observe your students engaged in the mathematics they are learning, will you provide oral feedback to students as they work, or will you use the tools provided in Figures 1.3, 1.4, or 1.6 to provide feedback at another time (perhaps at the end of the lesson or even the end of the day)?

questions, while the next section of the chapter presents actual tools (Figures 1.2 and 1.3) you can use to help guide your planning of the observation as well as monitor what may actually occur and what you might notice as the lesson is implemented.

Grade 1: Lesson focus is: counting to 120, starting at any number less than 120. In this range, read and write numerals and represent a number of objects with a written numeral. Consider the following as you plan such a lesson.

What would you expect to observe?

- Would you expect to see and hear students orally counting from a given number (e.g., orally counting from 71 to 120)?

- Would you expect to see students representing given numbers and a counting sequence using base-ten rods (e.g., represent 71 and count on using base-ten rods from that number)?

- Would you anticipate orally hearing a counting sequence long enough that you could determine that students could orally count to 120 or another designated number from a given starting point (e.g., start with 83 and count to 105)?

- **Your turn:** What else might you anticipate observing? And, given YOUR class, YOUR students, what might YOU expect to observe?

How would you know "it" if you saw it?

- You would see and hear students counting on from a given number.

- You would see appropriate use of base-ten materials as students counted on from a given number to an end number, perhaps 120.

- You would hear varied but appropriate counting sequences as you observed.

- **Your turn:** What other "its" might you see and/or hear?

What mathematical challenges or misconceptions might you observe?

- Students confused as to the "start number" (e.g., starting at zero rather than an identified start number)

- Students unable to write numbers

- Students challenged when counting orally and bridging from one decade to the next

- Students challenged when using representations (models) for two- or three-digit numbers

- **Others?** What particular misconceptions have you seen/experienced that may occur?

How might you record and provide feedback of what you observe?

- Consider the examples of the individual student, small group, and class observation tools found on pages 32–38. You can access these tools for your own use at **http://resources.corwin.com/Formative5.**

- Consider taking a picture of what you observe as a record of student performance.

- Consider an observed response that may require immediate oral (typically) feedback.

- Consider use of a brief comment from your records as feedback provided later in the day or at some other time— perhaps within a parent/teacher conference.

Grade 3: Lesson focus is: representing a fraction $\frac{a}{b}$ on a number line diagram by marking off a lengths $\frac{1}{b}$ from 0. Recognize that the resulting interval has the size $\frac{a}{b}$ and that its endpoint locates the number $\frac{a}{b}$ on the number line. Consider the following as you plan such a lesson.

What would you expect to observe?

- Would you expect to see students representing fractions on the number line by iterating the unit fraction (e.g., show $\frac{3}{4}$ by noting 3 lengths of $\frac{1}{4}$)?
- Would you expect to see students comfortable when creating and labeling unit fraction iterations on their number lines?
- Would you want to orally hear how students determined and plotted the location of fractions as requested?
- **Your turn:** What else might you hope to observe? And, given YOUR class, YOUR students, what might YOU expect to observe?

How would you know "it" if you saw it?

- You would see and hear students plotting particular fractions on their number lines based on the interval of the assigned fraction(s).

- You would see appropriate use of the number line as a representational tool and linear (measurement) model for fractions.

- **Your turn:** What other "its" might you see and/or hear?

What mathematical challenges or misconceptions might you observe?

- Students having difficulty plotting fractions on the number line by counting unit fractions

- Students lacking experience in the use of the number line as a representational tool

- **Others?** What particular misconceptions have you seen/ experienced that may occur?

How might you record and provide feedback of what you observe?

- Consider the examples of the individual student, small group, and class observation tools found on pages 32–38. You can access these tools for your own use at **http://resources.corwin.com/Formative5.**

- Consider taking a picture of what you observe as a record of student performance.

- Consider an observed response that may require immediate oral (typically) feedback.

- Think about how you might provide feedback to your students using your responses to the Planning for Observations questions (Figure 1.1).

Grade 5: Lesson focus is: interpret division of a unit fraction by a nonzero whole number, and compute such quotients. Demonstrate by creating a word problem for $\frac{1}{2} \div 4 = \frac{1}{8}$ because $\frac{1}{8} \times 4 = \frac{1}{2}$, and representing the solution using a visual model. Consider the following as you plan such a lesson.

What would you expect to observe?

- Would you expect to see students working together, in small groups, as they create their word problems?

- Would you truly hope to see students creating a word problem that was not about pizza?

- Would you expect to see students using the number line or an area model to partition $\frac{1}{2}$ by 4 (dividing by 4)?

- Would you anticipate that students would recognize that $\frac{1}{2} \div 4 = \frac{1}{8}$ since $\frac{1}{8} \times 4$ or $\frac{4}{8} = \frac{1}{2}$?

- **Your turn:** What else might you expect to observe? And, given YOUR class, YOUR students, what might YOU expect to observe?

How would you know "it" if you saw it?

- You would see and hear students sharing word problems for $\frac{1}{2} \div 4 = \frac{1}{8}$, plotting particular fractions on their number lines based on the interval of the assigned fraction(s).

- In addition to an appropriate word problem, you would see students use manipulatives, an area model, or the number line to represent the problem and solution for $\frac{1}{2} \div 4 = \frac{1}{8}$ recognizing that $\frac{1}{2} \div 4 = \frac{1}{8}$ can be thought of as $4 \times \frac{1}{8} = \frac{1}{2}$.

- **Your turn:** What other "its" might you see and/or hear?

What mathematical challenges or misconceptions might you observe?

- Students having difficulty framing word problem contexts for $\frac{1}{2} \div 4 = \frac{1}{8}$

- Students unable to recognize the relationship between $\frac{1}{2} \div 4 = \frac{1}{8}$ and $\frac{1}{8} \times 4 = \frac{1}{2}$

- Students having limited experience using representations for division of fraction problems

- Students more comfortable using area models than the number line for representing division of fraction problems

- **Others?** What particular misconceptions have you seen/ experienced that may occur?

How might you record and provide feedback of what you observe?

- Consider the examples of the individual student, small group, and class observation tools found on pages 32–38. You can access these tools for your own use at **http://resources.corwin.com/Formative5.**

- Consider taking a picture of what you observe as a record of student performance.

- Consider an observed response that may require immediate oral (typically) feedback.

- Think about how you might provide feedback to your students using your responses to the Planning for Observations questions (Figure 1.1).

Grade 7: Lesson focus is: decide whether two quantities are in a proportional relationship. Test for equivalent ratios by using a ratio table or graphing on a coordinate plane and observing whether the graph is a straight line through the origin. Consider the following as you plan such a lesson.

What would you expect to observe?

- Would you hope to see that students recognize how earlier understandings related to fraction equivalence is related to determining proportional relationships?

- Would you expect to see students comfortably using ratio tables to represent and help create equal ratios/ proportions?

- Would you expect to see students using coordinate graphs to represent and then define proportional relationships?

- **Your turn:** What else might you hope to observe? And, given YOUR class, YOUR students, what might YOU expect to observe?

How would you know "it" if you saw it?

- You would see students using ratio tables to create proportions.

- Students would accurately describe how they created or validated proportional relationships using the ratio table and/or the coordinate plane.

- **Your turn:** What other "its" might you see and/or hear?

What mathematical challenges or misconceptions might you observe?

- Students having difficulty connecting equivalent fraction understandings to proportional relationships

- Students not being comfortable in their use of the ratio table or coordinate plane

- Students not understanding how to create and recognize proportional relationships

- **Others?** What particular misconceptions have you seen/ experienced that may occur?

How might you record and provide feedback of what you observe?

- Consider the examples of the individual student, small group, and class observation tools found on pages 32–38. You can access these tools for your own use at **http://resources.corwin.com/Formative5.**

- Consider taking a picture of what you observe as a record of student performance.

- Consider an observed response that may require immediate oral (typically) feedback.

- Think about how you might provide feedback to your students using your responses to the Planning for Observations questions (Figure 1.1).

The grade-level examples above are all somewhat related in that they demonstrate how you might consider use of the questions provided in Figure 1.1 as you plan for using observation within a particular lesson. Note that the particular considerations for an observation with regard to what you expect to observe, how you would know "it" if you saw it, and anticipated mathematical challenges or misconceptions will vary with the content focus of the lesson and the prior knowledge of your students.

Tools for Using Observations in the Classroom

The tools provided in this section of the chapter should assist you as you plan for and regularly use observation as a formative assessment technique. The tools are related to planning for using observation, and monitoring small group, class, and individual student observations, and presented accordingly. Figure 1.2 will assist in your planning. This tool is useful for responding to the questions provided in the previous section of this chapter regarding your observation expectations. An example of how this tool can be used is provided using the Grade 5 lesson example discussed previously. You may access a blank version of this tool at **http://resources.corwin.com/Formative5.**

Figure 1.3 is a tool that was derived from our ongoing work and collaboration with school and classroom-based mathematics leaders, who have found that it is most helpful as a recording tool that can be used to make note of what's observed. It is also helpful for documentation of student responses, which can then be accessed for providing feedback to a small group of students, although this tool could also be used to record observation of individual students. Figure 1.3 is an actual example of how the Implementation and Recording Tool can be used. You can decide to carry this around and just jot down comments about what you observe, as some do, or at the end of the day, you can reflect on what you observed. Either way, this tool provides a record of you monitoring whatever

Figure 1.2 • Planning: Observations Template

Mathematics Standard: Grade 5: Division of a unit fraction by a whole number

Lesson Objective: Interpret division of a unit fraction by a nonzero whole number, and compute such quotients.

What would you expect to observe?	How would you know "it" if you saw it?	What mathematical challenges or misconceptions might you observe?	How might you record and provide feedback of what you observe?
Students solving the following problem using drawings: Edgar had $\frac{1}{2}$ of an apple pie. It was shared by 4 people. How much pie did each person have to eat? Use drawings to show your solution.	I would expect to see a circular or rectangular region showing $\frac{1}{2}$ then cut or shared by 4, with each slice labeled $\frac{1}{8}$.	I know some of my students struggle with drawing representations when doing operations with fractions.	I may take a picture of several problem solutions and have the students show and discuss them with the class.

Images: Clipart.com

A blank template version of this figure is available for download at
http://resources.corwin.com/Formative5

elements of your lesson you want to document. Some teachers may use this tool for comments about the class as a whole, but we have observed that most like to use it for observing a particular small group of students or individual students. You can download this tool at **http://resources.corwin.com/Formative5**.

Figure 1.4 is a tool that allows you to keep an observation record for all students individually. It does not provide the opportunity to describe what you have observed in depth like Figure 1.3, but it does allow for a brief comment and—perhaps more importantly— provides you with a quick way to monitor all of your students.

Figure 1.3 • Small Group: Implementation and Recording Tool for Observations

Intent of the Observation	Brief Description/ Comments	Observed?
Mathematics Content	Students (4 of 5) successfully representing equivalent fractions on the number line; one student in this group really struggling.	Yes, for 4 of 5 students; I need to set up an interview with one student.
Mathematical Practices	Reasoning, using tools	Yes, but several of the students seemed just a little unsure about getting started with the number lines.
Student Engagement	Using the number line, a small group of 5 students were to represent 4 fractions equivalent to $\frac{1}{2}$ and discuss how they represented the equivalent fractions.	I think I may need to spend a little more time tomorrow discussing their reasoning for placing the fractions on the number line and equivalence, in general.

General Comment: Overall, this group seemed to do pretty well with this activity. I need to work more directly with one student who seems lost. I also need to help the group, maybe even my whole class, on just constructing number lines.

Feedback to Students: I will be interviewing one of the students and then talking briefly to the other 4 as a group. I quickly checked each of the student number lines and asked for a validation of what they did and why—pleased with their response, particularly for a second lesson involving equivalent fractions.

Source: Fennell, F., Kobett, B., & Wray, J. (2015). Classroom-based formative assessments: Guiding teaching and learning. In C. Suurtamm (Ed.) & A. McDuffie (Series Ed.), *Annual perspectives in mathematics education: Assessment to enhance teaching and learning* (pp. 51–62). Reston, VA: National Council of Teachers of Mathematics. Republished with permission of the National Council of Teachers of Mathematics; permission conveyed through Copyright Clearance Center, Inc.

A blank template version of this figure is available for download at
http://resources.corwin.com/Formative5

It can be used for one day; several days, as noted below; or the entire week. Note that the comments on the observation checklist (Figure 1.4) are quick notes. The advantage to this tool is that it's quite efficient to use, and it allows you to observe and record

Figure 1.4 • Classroom: Observation Checklist

Unit: Grade 4: Operations and Algebraic Thinking			Date: 2/7 to 2/10
Lesson Focus: Three days: Problem solving with whole numbers; factors and multiples; patterns			
Student Name	**Math Focus**	**Math Focus**	**Math Focus**
	2/7 Use the four operations with whole numbers to solve problems.	2/9 Gain familiarity with factors and multiples.	2/10 Generate and analyze patterns.
Anthony	On task, doing well	On task, slow start	He's got this—very pleased with himself.
Barbara	On task, struggling just a bit	Struggling; need to interview ASAP—today!	Interview coming up on this topic too, will need to do this tomorrow
Joe	Completed the task quickly; need to provide a more challenging follow-up example	Liked this, he's engaged. Today's tasks worked better than the previous lesson.	Doing fine
Angela	On task	On task	On task
Cynda	On task	For the most part on task	On task
Bryce	On task, but management issues within her group	Knows I'm watching, more focused than earlier	On task, management is no longer an issue
Matt	Doing well	Continues to do well	Has had a great day
Chris	Struggling	Need to interview and possibly do Show Me with him	May not get to this today
Mia	Need to work with individually ASAP	Did not start this activity—not ready	Will do this tomorrow
Janet	Disrupting progress of her group	Settled down, working pretty well in a paired activity	Doing fine
Add more rows as needed to accommodate all members of the class.			

A blank template version of this figure is available for download at
http://resources.corwin.com/Formative5

comments about as many of the students in your class as you would like. Access this tool from **http://resources.corwin.com/ Formative5** and adapt it to your needs.

The Classroom: Observation—Student Representations tool (Figure 1.5), which is adapted from the work of Smith and Stein (2011), is specifically focused on observing student use of varied representations, which is critically important in the development of understanding of major mathematics concepts in Grades K–8. This tool allows you to track anticipated and observed use of representations as well as who uses particular representations, also suggesting the order in which you may want students to share their representations and how they used them to solve problems. Finally, this classroom-based observation tool will provide you with information regarding student use and related understandings of

Figure 1.5 • Classroom: Observation—Student Representations

Student Representations (Anticipated/ Observed)	Who Is Using Specific Representations	Who I Will Select to Share Their Representations (order of presentations; 1st, 2nd, . . .)
Anticipated: Base ten block modeling		
Observed: Base ten block modeling	Ralph, Eric, Paige, Mia	1st—Mia; 2nd—Paige
Observed: Student pictures/drawings	Adrianna, Jazzmin, Katie, Heather, Bryce, Justin	3rd—Katie; 4th—Justin
Observed: Response to the task was accurate; representations were not used	Fran, Brett, Simone, Karen	5th—Simone; 6th—Brett
Observed: No representation provided, incorrect response to the problem	Timmy	This is important information. I will interview Timmy to assess his challenges with the task. For now, I will not have him share.

Source: Adapted from Smith, M. S., & Stein, M. K. (2011). *5 practices for orchestrating productive mathematics discussions.* Reston, VA: National Council of Teachers of Mathematics.

 A blank template version of this figure is available for download at
http://resources.corwin.com/Formative5

varied representations, including manipulative materials, drawings, particular representations used with and for whole numbers as well as fraction representations, and so on.

The intent of the Individual Student: Mathematics Strengths Observation Log (Figure 1.6) is to document observations for individual students in greater depth. Note that this tool accounts for areas of a student's progress that includes mathematical disposition, how memory may play a part of a student's response, a student's attention to elements of the mathematics experienced, socioemotional elements of the learner, and organizational skills. You would use the Mathematics Strengths Observation Log in the following way:

- **Mathematics Concepts/Skills:** Record what you have observed mathematics-wise in the lesson or lessons recently observed.

- **Mathematical Disposition:** Note that the example response indicates how the student approaches the mathematics learning opportunities of the day.

- **Memory:** Discuss the extent to which the student's memory may have impacted responses. This will be more of a consideration for particular lessons (e.g., vocabulary, basic and related facts, mental mathematics).

- **Attention:** Consider the student's attention to the activities presented. Note the comment related to Maria's attention.

- **Socioemotional:** Address the student's ability and willingness to get along with others, persist in solving problems, and otherwise engage in the mathematics being presented.

- **Organizational:** Note how this element of the tool addresses how well the student is organized to attend to the demands of the mathematics activities central to the lesson.

As noted, you would consider this tool for an individual student you are closely observing, particularly a student for whom a more complete picture of progress may be needed. Our experience has been that many teachers like to use the Individual Student: Mathematics Strengths Observation Log in conjunction with or as an interview (Chapter 2). Some teachers also like to use this log to collect observed student strengths over time.

The Observation Check-In (Figure 1.7) is a tool that teachers with whom we work like to use for a quick "check-in" for individual students. Often placed on a tablet or 3 × 5 card, teachers can move around the classroom and just circle the extent to which individual

Figure 1.6 • Individual Student: Mathematics Strengths Observation Log

Mathematics Strengths Observation Log for: Maria, Grade 2					Date: 3/14	
	Learner Profile					
Mathematics Concepts/ Skills	**Mathematical Disposition**	**Memory**	**Attention**	**Socioemotional**	**Organizational Skills**	
List the student strengths with specific content, concepts, and skills.	What types of content, tasks, and activities does the student respond to with positivity, interest, and engagement?	What kinds of things does the student remember?	What strengths does the student demonstrate? Does the student attend to particular types of activities?	How well does the student: • Work with others? • Productively struggle? • Persist?	How does the student organize/ record thinking for mathematics?	
Maria does well with activities involving counting and place value.	Maria seems interested in today's lesson and is generally interested in mathematics and almost always fully engaged. She does seem to get frustrated with problems involving the situations for addition and subtraction.	Memory is not a factor in today's lesson, but does seem to slow Maria up on math fact lessons. Maria seems to remember content best when connected to a real-world context.	Maria was focused for most of today's lesson, but she seemed to move a little too quickly through one of the lesson's final problems. Maria seems to attend best at the beginning of a lesson and during discussions and group work.	Maria was really engaged in the group task today. She led the group in recording responses.	Maria needed help getting organized in today's lesson. She organizes her work best when I help her set up a plan before she starts working.	

A blank template version of this figure is available for download at
http://resources.corwin.com/Formative5

Figure 1.7 • Individual Student: Observation Check-In

Name: Roberto	Date: March 14
Mathematics Focus of the Lesson: Adding unit fractions	

Elements of the Lesson (Early, Mid, End)	Productively Engaged	
Early: Using the number line to add unit fractions, with sums < 1	(Yes)	No
Mid-Lesson: Discussion of student number line drawings	(Yes)	No
End of the Lesson: Move to symbolically adding unit fractions	Yes	(No)
Need for an interview?	(Yes)	No

Comments: Roberto was engaged for most of the lesson and seemed to do well until we reached the examples where he was actually adding fractions (e.g., $\frac{1}{2} + \frac{1}{2}$). Will see how he does in tomorrow's lesson, which will continue with addition of unit fractions and move to subtraction of unit fractions. I think I will do a brief interview with Roberto toward the end of tomorrow's lesson.

A blank template version of this figure is available for download at
http://resources.corwin.com/Formative5

students or a small group of students is productively engaged in the lesson at various stages of the lesson: early, midway, and end of the lesson. You can also indicate if you would like to extend the observation to include an interview and provide comments related to what you have observed. This functional, easy-to-use tool indicates the extent to which your students are engaged in what you have planned, which is important for your planning the next day and beyond.

Consider the following questions and classroom-based responses as helpful suggestions on how you might use the tools presented in Figures 1.2–1.7.

1. **Lots of tools, just for observation here. I'm not expected to use all of these, all the time, right? I'm not even sure where to start!**

   Classroom-Based Response: *When I first began thinking hard about how to not just observe what my students were* *doing in mathematics class each day but also connect to my planning and begin to record what I had observed, Figure 1.2, Planning: Observations Template, became my new best friend! The questions on what I then called my planning tool (Figure 1.2) are pretty basic, and use of this tool really helped me get started in thinking about how to truly consider how and even when to use observation as an assessment technique.*

2. **Which of these tools should I use and when?**

   Classroom-Based Response: *I had never recorded much of anything I observed my students doing in mathematics class! Boy, has the study and use of the Formative 5 changed my view. I was always grasping for comments at parent/ teacher conferences or when I received calls from parents, and I seemingly never had actual "evidence" of what my students were doing or had done. The more I got into seriously reviewing and actually trying out the tools provided for observation, the more I realized that they were organized as small group (Figure 1.3), class (Figures 1.4 and 1.5), or individual student (Figures 1.6 and 1.7) observation tools. I started with the small group tool (Figure 1.3), since my independent work stations were organized by small groups. This tool worked well for me. Lately, I have been using the classroom observation tool, which focuses on the use of representations, since my work with fractions really emphasizes varied representations. This works well too and allows me to bounce between use of the small group tool, which I am now very comfortable with, and this whole class observation tool, which is focused on representations. I have also discovered that these tools are very valuable for parent conferences. They provide me with explicit data over time, which helps me explain student mathematical understandings to parents. They love it!*

3. **How much of what I observe should I actually record, and when?**

   Classroom-Based Response: *I have found that once I considered what I would observe as I planned my lesson, it was easier to determine which of the observation tools I would use, and that influenced how much I would record. In general, I would take notes on a tablet as I moved around the room. Sometimes I used the Classroom: Observation Checklist (Figure 1.4) for a full week, or at minimum several days, so I could see if there were tendencies being exhibited by particular students—having particular mathematical* *difficulties, not paying attention, and so on. Sometimes I would add more to my comments after mathematics class or at the end of the day. If I had particular concerns about what a student was doing, it almost always drove me to use one of the two individual student observation tools. Figure 1.6, Individual Student: Mathematics Strengths Observation Log, really examines a variety of learning dimensions that have always been helpful for me to document before I consider an interview for a student, and it requires more documentation than Figure 1.7, Individual Student: Observation Check-In, which is a quick response tool that essentially monitors student engagement at key points throughout the lesson. Not always, but often, what I have observed using the small group (Figure 1.3) or classroom tools (Figures 1.4 and 1.5) suggested the use of one of the two individual observation tools (Figures 1.6 and 1.7). After almost a year of truly using observation as a valued formative assessment technique, I know I am much more comfortable in deciding which observation tools to use, and when and how much to record, all of which provides me with suggestions for the feedback I can give to my students and particular next steps, which may be an interview.*

Technology Tips and Tools for Recording Observations

In addition to the above, there are some digital tools that provide teachers with the means to capture student observations, each of which has specific advantages. As with any digital tool that is used to collect student data, be sure to investigate and follow school district data privacy policies and practices, and communicate the privacy plan and purpose of your recordings with parents/guardians and students:

- Virtually every digital handheld smartphone or tablet device comes equipped with a digital still image and video camera. The images and videos collected during your observations of students can allow both you and your students to document and review the following: student engagement with various mathematical practices, use of representations, mathematical arguments and reasoning, and preconceptions and/or misconceptions—all evidence of student learning. The digital files can be easily captured, stored, and used as powerful formative artifacts for students and teachers, and inform plans for next steps.

Having opportunities to pause, analyze, and re-experience an observation captured digitally, rather than relying on memory or written notes, can be extremely beneficial.

- Google Forms (http://www.google.com/forms) can be used to create your own classroom observation look-fors. This free and easy-to-use resource can be an effective and efficient way of capturing observation data and seamlessly accessing them in spreadsheet form for later analysis.

Using Observations in YOUR Classroom

When thinking about the use of observations to guide and monitor planning and instruction in YOUR classroom, consider the following:

When do I do this? When should I use observation? How do I use these tools in concert with one another? Expect to observe every day to inform your teaching and guide your planning. As noted in the previous section of this chapter, the observation tools provided in the chapter are potentially helpful to you initially as you plan for observing (Figure 1.2) and then as you consider observations with and for small groups of students (Figure 1.3), classroom observation (Figures 1.4 and 1.5), and observing individual students (Figures 1.6 and 1.7). The more you directly consider how and what you will observe and its importance in the planning, teaching, assessment cycle, the less you will have to think about it. What and how you observe, and use of the tools noted previously, will become an integral component of your planning and teaching.

Your observations will range from relatively quick and informal observations to focused, deliberate observations of individual students (see Figures 1.6 and 1.7), small groups (see Figure 1.3), or the entire class (see Figures 1.4 and 1.5). When planning, as you consider what you anticipate or expect to observe, your observations will become a natural, seamless way in which you take notice of what students are doing mathematically and use that information to guide and monitor student and class progress. Consider the following as you plan for and use observations.

- Focus on observing content understandings and student engagement with particular Standards for Mathematical Practice (e.g., reasoning, problem solving, precision, modeling with mathematics).

While you will, no doubt, observe off-task or distracting conduct/behavior as your students engage in a mathematics activity, try not to be overly distracted by such student behaviors. Take the time to make note of these behaviors as they accumulate and attend to them as needed. It will be important to consider if and how such behavior may be impacting a student's performance in mathematics. Observing, perhaps even informally timing, how long students stay on task with regard to completing a mathematics problem or related assignments may be one way to judge the impact of behaviors on mathematics performance. Some teachers make a note on the Small Group: Implementation and Recording Tool for Observations (Figure 1.3) or one of the two classroom observations tools (Figures 1.6 and 1.7), noting when and how frequently off-task and distracting behaviors actually occur. We also note that students who don't understand and are unsure of expectations may be more likely to be off task, however defined, than others.

- Remember the intent of the observation. The observation should be intentionally connected to the actual planning and implementation of the day's lesson. This is a key point.

- This is YOUR classroom. Expect a full range of responses. Recognize when students are challenged, when they seemingly "sail through" an activity, or when they exhibit signs of frustration.

- *Principles to Actions* (NCTM, 2014) notes that effective teaching of mathematics engages students in solving and discussing tasks that promote mathematical reasoning and problem solving. This is another key point directly related to your planning and to the use of observation as a formative assessment technique. How can observations be used to validate the level of engagement you desire? Note that the Individual Student: Observation Check-In tool (Figure 1.7) addresses the extent to which students are engaged at key points throughout a lesson.

- Document, document, document. Keeping a record and analysis of what is observed will more directly inform decisions during the lesson's implementation and advise your short-term and long-term planning. The observation tools (Figures 1.2–1.7) presented and discussed earlier are all classroom tested and can be electronically adapted to meet your observation needs. Visit **http://resources .corwin.com/Formative5** to gain access to templates for the observation tools.

- Anticipate what might be observed. As you plan, what do you expect your students to do? That's what will be observed. Connecting observations to your everyday planning allows you to not only monitor your instruction, but, perhaps more importantly, anticipate or even imagine what will happen in your lesson, and adapt accordingly.

Summing Up

As a classroom-based formative assessment technique, the observation provides that initial link to planning and instruction. It allows you to consider, before the lesson is taught, what students will do, how they might engage in the mathematics, possible lesson products, issues related to student grouping, differentiation, and much more. The potential of this preteaching "look for" or noticing opportunity should influence your planning—every day. Additionally, what you actually observe within a lesson should be the catalyst for the next lesson's planning and instruction and will provide day-to-day anecdotal indicators of student progress and help you make the most of your lesson. Anticipating what you will observe will help you to determine lesson activities, problem-based tasks, and questions. Utilize the observation tools presented and discussed in this chapter (Figures 1.2–1.7). Records of what's observed will provide a pattern of student performance that is useful for monitoring progress, providing feedback to students, or guiding conferences with parents/family and others. Keeping a record of observations should also influence the pace of your lessons and decision making within a lesson, as well as provide indicators for additional longer term planning and instruction. Finally, your use of observations on a regular basis will identify the need for the regular use of interviews, the second element of the Formative 5 palette of classroom-based formative assessment techniques.

Professional Learning Discussion Questions

Read and discuss the following questions with your grade-level teaching team or with teams across multiple grade levels. Take notes here or use the tools in the Book Study Guide to record your thoughts.

How often do you actually use observation? Would you consider your use of observation as formative assessment?

How might you use observation every day to monitor your students as you teach and as they learn mathematics?

In thinking about what you expect to observe, also think about how you would know "it" (what you expect) when you saw it. What will you do if you don't see "it," or students don't do what you expect?

When would you actually make notes about what you have observed in your mathematics classroom?

Which of the observation tools in this chapter might you use or adapt and use in your own classroom? What observation tools have you created or used?

Notes

_____

_____

_____

_____

_____

_____

_____

_____

_____

_____

_____

_____

_____

_____

_____

_____

_____

_____

_____

_____

_____

_____

_____

_____

_____

_____

_____

> **"** I observe and talk with my students all day long every single day. Now I know how to formalize my comments and conduct an interview. So powerful! **"**

—KINDERGARTEN TEACHER

> **"** For some reason I thought that you only interviewed students who were having problems in math class. Now I regularly interview my algebra students because I want to assess how they are transitioning to using equations and inequalities in a more formal way. **"**

—EIGHTH-GRADE TEACHER

CHAPTER 2
INTERVIEWS

Interviews: Background and Basics

The use of the interview as an assessment technique has a long history and includes connections to both mathematics and special education (Fennell, 1998, 2011; Ginsburg, 1997; Weaver, 1955). A brief one-on-one or small group interview has the potential to yield cues regarding particular mathematical challenges, misconceptions, shallow understanding, and cues for next steps instructionally. Years ago, Weaver (1955) noted that interviewing children allows teachers to study levels of student thinking as they respond to a variety of quantitative situations. Ginsburg (1997) suggests that the use of a clinical interview can follow what a teacher initially observes regarding a written or oral response. Such observed responses are then followed up with questions to engage the child in discussing the "how and why" of their solution strategies. An important component of the Formative 5, the interview can be thought of as an informal conversation between teacher and student, or perhaps a small group of students. Interview questions may be as informal as "How did you do that?" "Why did you do it that way?" or "Can you explain how you solved that?" (Ginsburg & Dolan, 2011). The use of the interview assumes that rapport between the teacher and student has been established. **Interviews** are extensions of observations. They are brief and informal conversations between the teacher and an individual or small group that provide a glimpse into student thinking. As conducted, interview questions encourage students to respond, but do not suggest a particular or expected response. For many reasons, mostly related to instructional time, the interview is usually brief, typically five minutes or less, sometimes up to ten minutes for a more in-depth interview. Consider the following example of how what's observed can suggest the need for an interview.

> Interviews are extensions of observations. They are brief and informal conversations between the teacher and an individual or small group of students that provide a glimpse into student thinking.

The day's lesson involved partitioning regarding fractions and mixed numbers. The students were asked to use materials or drawings to show how they could share eleven cookies with four students, and $\frac{1}{2}$ of a large cake among three students. Janet's response is provided in Figures 2.1 and 2.2. What Janet did was quite interesting as her representations differ for each of the problems. For sharing eleven cookies with four students, she circled two cookies four times, so everybody got at least two cookies. Then she divided two of the remaining cookies in half and gave a half cookie to each of the four students—so each now had $2\frac{1}{2}$ cookies. Finally, she divided the last cookie into fourths, giving an additional $\frac{1}{4}$ cookie to each of the four students. So each student now had $2\frac{3}{4}$ cookies.

When Janet used a drawing to show how she shared $\frac{1}{2}$ of the large cake among three students, she drew a rectangular cake and then divided into thirds, indicating that each student would get $\frac{1}{3}$ of the cake.

Figure 2.1 • Janet's Solution—Sharing Eleven Cookies With Four Students

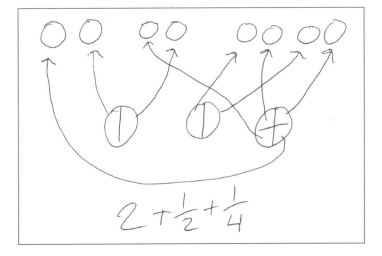

Figure 2.2 • Janet's Solution: Sharing $\frac{1}{2}$ of a Cake Among Three Students

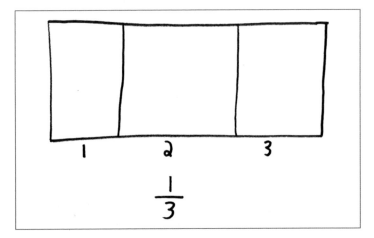

Given Janet's response to the lesson's tasks, would you want to discuss what she did in an interview during the lesson or perhaps some other time that day? What questions might you consider asking Janet? Responses like Janet's are why you might use an interview. Such responses provide you with an opportunity to explore student thinking and understanding and may also be used to jump-start planning and related activities for tomorrow's mathematics lesson.

Planning for the Interview

Our motivation for including the interview technique as one of the Formative 5 is that it provides the obvious follow-up to an observation or observations you may make when implementing a lesson. This classroom-based interview, which is an adaptation of a more clinical interview, allows, even suggests, that you spend a few valuable minutes digging deeper with an individual student or perhaps a small group of students. While some immediately think about the practical issues regarding how and when to find time to actually conduct interviews, our experience confirms how flexible teachers can be once they recognize the utility and impact of the interview. Consider the following comments:

> At first, I had no idea when I would be able to actually do the interview during the hubbub and buzz of my math time. Then I just created this 'you and me' spot in the corner of the room and when I observed something I wanted to ask about, I just said, 'It's you and me time, right now.' The kids really seem to look forward to it. It's kind of like their private math time with me! I did try hard to make the interviews about five minutes or so long and took brief notes on what was discussed. Valuable technique—use it every day!
>
> —FIRST-GRADE TEACHER

> I loved the potential of interviews, but I worried about when I might actually conduct them and I did not want to wait until the end of the day. So, I use small group interviews—right around my work table. I do this every day usually based on responses I observe that are pretty similar, but not always. The group sharing of my questions works well for me and it really helps me plan for individual and class needs.
>
> —THIRD-GRADE TEACHER

INTERVIEWS

> ❝ I had never even considered using an interview as a type of formative assessment. As I learned about the potential of a brief interview, sort of extending what I observed, I tried it. Now, as I observe students when I get them involved in newer concepts in prealgebra, I use the individual interview tool (Figure 2.6) either during my class or during transition time between my classes. My interviews are short, probably two to three minutes, but particularly helpful in determining what my students can do and helping me think about topics that may need more time instructionally. ❞
>
> —EIGHTH-GRADE TEACHER

Jake's 3 + 4 = 8 Interview

http://resources
.corwin.com/Formative5

To read a QR code, you must have a smartphone or tablet with a camera. We recommend that you download a QR code reader app that is made specifically for your phone or tablet brand.

Jake's 21 + 23 Interview

http://resources
.corwin.com/Formative5

Jake's 35 + 49 Interview

http://resources
.corwin.com/Formative5

One thing that we have found in our continuing work with the interview technique is the need to communicate that use of the interview is not based on a deficit model. While you may want to interview a student based on a particular misconception or series of mathematical errors you observe, you may also want to interview a student because of a particularly unique or advanced response, or perhaps a response you just don't understand—and we have all seen our share! But why do this? The interview provides insights about student thinking that will inform your planning and instruction, allowing you the opportunity to adjust your planning and instruction to address needs more appropriately.

Consider the interview with Jake. Jake was somewhat new to the class and had missed a few days, so his teacher started out with the equation 3 + 4 = 8 and asked if it was true or false. Listen to Jake's response by scanning the first QR code on this page.

Then listen to his response to 21 + 23 = 100 and 35 + 49 = 100 by scanning the next two QR codes.

Note that in all three examples, Jake was just asked to indicate if the number sentence was true or false, but the responses yielded much more about what Jake knew and his thinking. As stated above, the comments Jake makes provide insights that his teacher can use as she plans her next lesson and as she plans for Jake.

As stated in the introductory chapter, your planning should include everyday attention to the Formative 5 techniques. As you consider the use of the interview, whether with one student or perhaps a small group of students, planning becomes an essential consideration. In this case, your planning will consider how what you expect to observe in the next day's lesson may warrant the use of an interview. The questions in Figure 2.3 should be helpful to you as you plan for an interview, keeping in mind, and as noted, that such a classroom-focused interview would be relatively brief.

Responses to the questions in Figure 2.3 should help you in considering the use of the interview as that next step beyond

Figure 2.3 • Planning for Interviews

1. Deciding on an Interview

- Who would you want to interview and why?
- Would you want to interview students one-on-one or in a small group?
- What might you have observed your students doing that would prompt the use of an interview?
- What will you consider when selecting students to interview related to their progress in a lesson? Would you think of a "sampling" of your students? That is, a student who may struggle with the day's lesson, one known for responses you never seem to expect or anticipate, and perhaps a student who you may want to challenge?

2. Setting Up Interviews

- Would you plan to complete the interview during the time you teach mathematics or sometime after the lesson?
- Where in the classroom would you conduct the interview?
- For particular areas of concern or interest, should you record the interview using video or audio, or perhaps use an interactive whiteboard app?
- How might you use physical and/or digital representation tools (e.g., base ten blocks, bar models, pattern blocks, number lines, and drawings) in the interview?

3. Interview Questions

- What questions might you ask?
- How might the questions differ for particular students?
- Would you ask students to discuss the "how and why" of what they did within a lesson activity?
- How could you personalize the interview? How could you pose questions so that students feel they are participating in a friendly, thoughtful, and helpful conversation rather than an interrogation?

4. Anticipating Interview Responses

- What responses might you anticipate from students? Would they show conceptual understandings? Would responses be related to procedures? Would they involve reasoning and sense making?
- To what extent do you think responses would reveal student mathematical dispositions?

5. Planning Follow-Up Questions

- What follow-up questions to particular student responses might you ask?
- Would such follow-up questions come at the end of the interview or later in the day?
- How might responses to the interview's follow-up questions influence your planning for the next day's lesson?

the observation. Interview questions may relate to a student's understanding of a mathematical concept, learning more about a particular strategy being used, extending student thinking, or assessing comprehension of a task to be solved. Depending on a student's response, follow-up questions can center on a variety of needs, such as the confidence level of the student in extending a response by taking it another direction (e.g., "Is your response reasonable? How do you know?").

Tools for Using Interviews in the Classroom

This chapter presents three tools for you to consider as you plan for and use the interview technique: a tool to assist you in planning for use of the interview, a tool to monitor your use of the interview with your class, and a tool for individual or perhaps small group interviews. Examples of the tools and comments by teachers who have used them follow the discussion of each tool. In addition, online tools helpful to you as you engage in everyday use of the interview technique are also presented.

The Planning: Interview Tool (Figure 2.4) is a useful guide to help plan for an interview as well as provide a record of student responses. The planning tool's elements are the consideration of the mathematics instructional goal or goals being assessed by the interview, whether you will be assessing conceptual understanding and/or procedural fluency, particular strategies being used, student prerequisites or misconceptions noticed, and the mathematical disposition of the student at particular times within or throughout the interview. We suggest that you complete and maintain a brief record of the student's response and your feedback to the student either during or right after the interview. The planning tool also provides space to record additional teacher comments or observations as well as general comments related to the interview and student responses. Note that archived interview comments will be helpful to your ongoing planning, guiding intervention efforts, and also as a source of day-to-day progress that may be useful within parent-teacher conferences. Download a blank version of this tool for your use at **http://resources.corwin.com/Formative5**.

1. **I wonder about planning a lesson and thinking about interviewing my students before I actually teach the lesson. I have NEVER done that before. How do I do this?**

   Classroom-Based Response: *I keep a copy of the Planning: Interview Tool (Figure 2.4) right next to me when I plan*

Figure 2.4 • Planning: Interview Tool

Mathematics Goal(s): *Grade 3: Fluently multiply and divide within 100, using strategies such as the relationship between multiplication and division or properties of operations.*

Assessing	Student Response	Feedback to Student(s)	Teacher Comments/ Observations
Conceptual Understanding	Asked Matt to use graph paper to show related multiplication and division products and quotients using shaded rectangles	Reviewed and provided oral and written feedback to Matt's rectangular region drawings and how they modeled multiplication and division	The graph paper activity worked well. Will use this again. Matt did well here—took a bit more time than I thought so we couldn't do that much, but I know he can do this independently—without me.
Procedural Fluency	Also asked Matt to orally state responses to triangular flash cards giving both multiplication and division responses (e.g., for 4, 5, 20: 4 × 5 = 20; 5 × 4 = 20; 20 ÷ 4 = 5; 20 ÷ 5 = 4)	Indicated which were correct or not orally, made a list of combinations needing further review	Matt was pretty quick and mostly accurate with the combinations reviewed. Will need more time for some combinations (6, 7, 42, 6, 8, 48, 8, 7, 56; 3, 8, 24)
Strategies Used	Matt didn't indicate the use of any strategies.		Need to ask Matt about his use of the commutative property, since he seemed not to understand how it could be used
Student Prerequisites and Misconceptions	No misconceptions observed. This is early work on multiplication, so I didn't observe any lack of prerequisites.		
Disposition	Seemed focused for most, but not all, of our time together	Talked to Matt about staying focused on the work	

General Comments: *Matt is doing well here. My next step is to provide him with an independent activity on the related facts he seemed to have difficulty with and those we didn't have time for. I will just observe how he does with this next step.*

Source: Adapted from Larson, M. R., Fennell, F., Adams, T. L., Dixon, J. K., Kobett, B. M., & Wray, J. A. (2012). *Common core mathematics in a PLC at work: Grades 3–5* (pp. 145, 146). Bloomington, IN. Adapted version published in C. Suurtamm (Ed.) & A. McDuffie (Series Ed.), *Annual perspectives in mathematics education: Assessment to enhance teaching and learning.* Reston, VA: National Council of Teachers of Mathematics.

 A blank template version of this figure is available for download at
http://resources.corwin.com/Formative5

my math lesson. I use it to look at my lesson (for tomorrow) and then think about what I might ask a student or students about what they are doing. I pay a lot of attention as to whether my "how or why" questions are about conceptual or procedural understandings. This is a helpful tool. I have made 4 × 6 file cards of the Planning: Interview Tool that I carry with me when I interview students. I make notes about student responses and my feedback and review each night before I plan.

An adaptation of the Planning: Interview Tool is the Classroom: Interview Record provided in Figure 2.5. Consider the Classroom: Interview Record as a way to quickly record interview responses for a group of students. When completed, the Classroom: Interview Record provides an at-a-glance view of group responses and potential needs. Download a blank version of this tool for your use at **http://resources.corwin.com/Formative5**.

2. **How can I get a quick sense of where my students, all of them, are regarding responses to my interview questions?**

    Classroom-Based Response: *I use the Classroom: Interview Record every day. A quick review of the student comments helps me when I think about groups for the next day's lesson. Maybe more important, at least for me, is that I have the whole class list in front of me on the Record and it keeps me alert as to who I have or haven't interviewed and who I have interviewed multiple times. I have found this tool to be a great record-keeping tool that allows me to track my interviews at a glance.*

The Individual Student: Interview Prompt (Figure 2.6) is a helpful resource that you can adapt to fit your needs and use to quickly record student responses to "how and why" questions you may ask during a brief interview designed to extend what you might see as you observe your students doing mathematics. Student interview responses can be filed journal-style and also used for planning related to the next day's lesson, plans for intervention, and so on. Download a blank version of this tool for your use at **http://resources.corwin.com/Formative5**.

3. **As I began to think about using the interview on a regular basis, I wondered about both how to keep a record of student responses to my interview questions and how I might be able to access my questions easily.**

Classroom-Based Response: *I like to use the Individual Student:*
Interview Prompt for particular students I might interview.
During math teaching time, I have the prompt questions on my
iPad so as I observe, I can be ready to do a short interview with
a few students. Sometimes I actually pull together a small group
and just ask them all to tell me how they solved a problem.

Figure 2.5 • Classroom: Interview Record

Student	Mathematics Content Focus	Mathematical Practice(s)	Learning Task	How did you solve that?	Why did you solve the problem that way?
Mia	Place value to 999	Reasoning, model with mathematics, use of tools	Compared two- and three-digit numbers	I used base ten blocks and then put them in order when comparing the numbers.	I don't know.
Cooper	Place value to 999	Reasoning, model with mathematics, use of tools	Compared two- and three-digit numbers	Just knew the larger numbers had the larger hundreds digit, and when the hundreds digit was the same I looked at the tens digit.	It was just easy for me to do it that way, sort of like thinking like a number line.

Add more rows as needed.

A blank template version of this figure is available for download at
http://resources.corwin.com/Formative5

INTERVIEWS

INTERVIEWS

Figure 2.6 • Individual Student: Interview Prompt

Interview Prompt*	
Name: Cassandra **Date:** 2/17 **Math Topic:** Division: one-digit divisors	
Question	**Student Responses**
1. How did you solve that?	I used base ten blocks to think through the first problem (147 ÷ 8), then I used the way we did these problems yesterday.
2. Why did you solve the problem that way?	It's how I usually do my division work.
3. What else can you tell me about what you did?	I thought it (and the other two problems) were all pretty easy to do.

*Note: Attach completed work sample(s).

A blank template version of this figure is available for download at
http://resources.corwin.com/Formative5

Technology Tips and Tools for Recording Interviews

There are some digital tools that provide teachers with the means to capture student interviews, each of which has specific advantages. As with any digital tool that is used to collect student data, be sure to investigate and follow school district data privacy policies and practices, and communicate the privacy plan and purpose of your recordings with parents/guardians and students:

- As with observations, video recording apps available on most digital handheld devices/tablets can be effectively used to capture and archive interview discussions with and among students. Of course, audio/voice recording apps or voice-to-text options on digital devices can also be used to capture or document interviews. These digital interview files can be easily shared with the whole class and can serve as a centerpiece for classroom discussion and debate, as well as the focus for professional learning conversations among teachers and teacher leaders.

- Some of the best tools to use include the following interactive whiteboard apps: Explain Everything™ (http://explaineverything.com), Educreations (https://www.educreations.com), ShowMe (http://www.showme.com), and Doceri (https://doceri.com). All four of these app-based tools allow the user to capture what is being represented and discussed during an interview on a digital whiteboard screen. With Explain Everything™, files can be easily captured and stored on the device and uploaded or shared via email, Dropbox, Google Drive, and so on.

Using Interviews in YOUR Classroom

When planning for the use of the interview in your classroom, recall that the interview extends what you might have observed. This means that just as you anticipate what you might observe as you plan a lesson, so should you consider particular elements of a lesson (e.g., a particular problem's solution, the first-time use of the number line to compare fractions) that, when observed, could suggest the need for an interview.

As you think about the structure of most, not all, interviews, it may be just asking a student to respond to a question or so about how he or she solved a problem and why he or she used a particular solution strategy to solve it. That is, the interview is based on something you have observed or expected to observe. We think of the following as "starter" statements and questions you may use to essentially turn what you are observing or have observed into an interview.

- How did you do that?
- Tell me why you did "that" (e.g., solved that problem) that way.
- Do you understand what you did?
- How would you explain what you did to a friend?

- I noticed that you stopped working on this problem a while ago. What happened?

- I noticed that you changed your answer. How come?

- Is there another way to solve this problem?

Of course, these "starter" statements and questions may be adapted to specific lesson tasks and the focus of what you have taught.

You can also consider providing your own separate task or activity solely for the interview with particular questions about this specific interview-created task. For example, the class could be working on comparing fractions on a number line, and your specific interview task might involve a problem like this:

Matt walked $\frac{3}{4}$ of the trail. If the trail was 8 miles long, how many miles did Matt walk? Interview questions related to this task could include the following:

- How could you (or did you) use a drawing or tool to represent this problem?

- How did you actually solve the problem?

- Do you think your answer is reasonable? How do you know?

- Did you think this problem was hard? Easy?

- Follow-up question: If the trail's length in miles was doubled, how long would $\frac{3}{4}$ of the trail be?

Note that the specifically designed interview task and related questions would need to be prepared and thought about either prior to a lesson or, and this is often the case when you want to dig deeper, as a response to what you expect to observe or have observed.

Generally speaking, when you consider use of the interview either to just extend what you have observed or as you specifically plan to use an interview with a student or group of students, think of the student! Well, of course, but here's what we mean. As you present a mathematical task or use questioning within the interview, make sure to allow the necessary time for the student(s) to process and respond *without* teacher intervention. While such intervention-like assistance is always well-intended, it sometimes, if not often, results in the teacher actually doing the mathematics rather than the student. Consider Robin's confession:

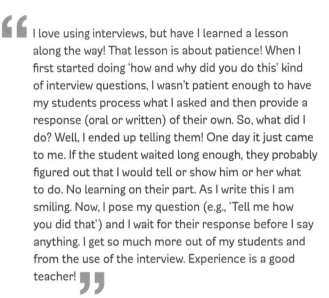

> I love using interviews, but have I learned a lesson along the way! That lesson is about patience! When I first started doing 'how and why did you do this' kind of interview questions, I wasn't patient enough to have my students process what I asked and then provide a response (oral or written) of their own. So, what did I do? Well, I ended up telling them! One day it just came to me. If the student waited long enough, they probably figured out that I would tell or show him or her what to do. No learning on their part. As I write this I am smiling. Now, I pose my question (e.g., 'Tell me how you did that') and I wait for their response before I say anything. I get so much more out of my students and from the use of the interview. Experience is a good teacher!
>
> —ROBIN, FIFTH-GRADE TEACHER

Most importantly, the interview as a classroom-based formative assessment technique extends what you observe, or expect to observe, as you continually strive to determine and monitor the progress of your students.

Summing Up

As noted, the interview provides you with the opportunity to dig deeper with regard to what you might observe within a lesson. As you plan, think hard about the purpose of your interview(s), including what you expect to learn and how interview responses may impact your planning for the next day and beyond. Interview responses provide potential identifiers for differentiation decisions, such as differentiating the pace of your lesson and differentiation plans for student groups and individual students. Also recognize that your understanding of the mathematics focus of the day's lesson and knowledge of your students should help to identify any lesson's "hot spots" that may prompt the actual use of the interview for particular students. Finally, regular consideration and use of the interview should augment your observations and help in recognizing the need to not only consider differentiation but also recognize potential mathematical challenges and misconceptions, explore areas of advanced understandings, and notice and address concerns related to student mathematical dispositions.

Professional Learning Discussion Questions

Read and discuss the following questions with your grade-level teaching team or with teams across multiple grade levels. Take notes here or use the tools in the Book Study Guide to record your thoughts.

Have you used interviews in your classroom? If so, how has their use impacted your planning and teaching?

What challenges do you envision as you think about daily use of the interview technique?

Which of the interview tools provided in this chapter would you use or adapt and use in your classroom?

How would you describe the link between your use of observation of mathematics teaching and the use of interviews in your classroom?

Think about one particular student you have and a very recent or forthcoming lesson. How would that student respond to the following interview questions?

How did you do that?

Tell me why you did "that" (e.g., solved that problem) that way.

Notes

_____

_____

_____

_____

_____

_____

_____

_____

_____

_____

_____

_____

_____

_____

_____

_____

_____

_____

_____

_____

_____

_____

_____

_____

_____

_____

> "Can you show me how you would order 76, 54, 47, and 89 using the number line?"

> "How do you know $\frac{3}{4}$ is less than $\frac{7}{8}$? Show me."

> "Show me your graph for that equation."

Show Me:
Background and Basics

We created the Show Me formative assessment technique because of the assessment potential of on-the-spot teacher prompts just like the ones above. Show Me was derived as we began to deeply consider, explore, and then implement the observation and interview techniques. What's a Show Me? A **Show Me** is a performance response by a student or group of students that extends and often deepens what was observed and what might have been asked within an interview. Its use is, to some extent, serendipitous and planned. Teachers are often caught off guard by or wonder about a student response and can ask a student to show what he or she did. Similarly, teachers can and should plan for particular elements within a lesson where Show Me may be warranted. The Show Me prompt requires a student or group of students to demonstrate their thinking and orally explain their response. And, like observations and interviews, Show Me is a classroom-based formative assessment technique, number three of the Formative 5, that, when used regularly, has the potential to not only monitor but also improve mathematics teaching and learning. This is particularly true because the use of Show Me supports and encourages differentiation.

Sueltz, Boynton, and Sauble (1946) recognized years ago that "observation, discussion, and interviews serve better than paper-pencil tests in evaluating a pupil's ability to understand the principles used" (p. 145). We recognized that, not unlike teacher use of observations, many teachers have probably asked their students to show them what they were doing, perhaps without recognizing the assessment value of such performance-based opportunities.

Shavelson, Baxter, and Pine (1992) noted that "a good assessment makes a good teaching activity and a good teaching activity makes a good assessment" (p. 22). Having your students show what they are doing or what you request them to do is such an activity/assessment. Show Me is interactive in that its use can provide an indication as to the extent to which what has been taught has been learned.

The National Council of Teachers of Mathematics' Assessment Standards (NCTM, 1995) note two important purposes of

Show Me is a performance response by a student or group of students that extends and often deepens what was observed and what might have been asked within an interview.

assessment that relate directly to use of the Show Me technique. These include the use of assessment to both monitor progress and inform instructional decisions. More recently, the National Mathematics Advisory Panel (2008) recommended research regarding "think alouds" in mathematics, which is a strategy typically used in reading and somewhat similar to what we propose in this chapter as Show Me.

Planning for Show Me

As noted above, Show Me is a performance-based response. It's essentially the on-the-spot extension of an observation or interview that deepens your understanding of what a student can do, which then suggests next steps for your planning and teaching. Deciding to ask a student or group of students to show seeks a demonstration of knowledge and understanding. Such responses help to identify or perhaps validate a level of progress in understanding or applying particular curricular standards within any of the mathematical content domains. Additionally, the very nature of a Show Me response will often address a number of Standards for Mathematical Practice (NGA Center & CCSSO, 2010). Show Me is a stop-and-drop, on-the-spot activity that should be relatively brief, less than five minutes. As noted, it's your extension of what you have observed or perhaps heard or saw within an interview. Consider Erin's commentary on the use of Show Me in her classroom.

> I was moving around and observing how my third-grade class was doing in creating drawings of a set of rectangles with the same perimeter but different areas and another set of rectangles with the same area, but different perimeters. I was watching Bryce work and wasn't at all sure I could understand her thinking, so I asked her to Show Me rectangles with a perimeter of 12. She zipped right through this showing 1 by 5, then 2 by 4, then 3 by 3 rectangles, noting that each had a perimeter of 12. And she talked me through each step of her work. However, when I asked her about the area of her rectangles, she wasn't at all sure about the area of any of her rectangles. I decided she needed a bit more of my time and that we would meet later and I would have her make the same rectangles, all with a perimeter of 12, using grid paper or tiles. That way, I could have her literally see the square units and determine the areas of her rectangles. I was glad I stopped what I was doing and

Show Me is a stop-and-drop, on-the-spot activity that should be relatively brief, less than five minutes.

SHOW ME

> had Bryce Show Me what she was doing and why. I also think Bryce's response may be somewhat representative of others in my class. I need to think about how my lesson tomorrow can draw the connections between like perimeters and area and like areas and perimeter. 🙲

Erin's use of Show Me was essentially an extension of what she observed. It revealed that Bryce seemed to understand the creation of rectangles with the same perimeter but was challenged by expressing the area of the rectangles. It also revealed the limitation of drawings and suggested the use of grid paper or tiles to represent the rectangles. Such models would provide the square units Bryce may need to determine the area of the rectangles she created.

Let's consider this Show Me response. Think about how you might be able to use it, if Bryce was your student. Bryce's responses truly advise Erin's planning for her lesson tomorrow. Our thinking is that Show Me truly demonstrates understandings and also reveals potential learning gaps that should inform instructional decisions. Importantly, such opportunities are most helpful in work with individual students or particular student groups. The questions in Figure 3.1 should be helpful to you as you both consider and complete preliminary planning for use of the Show Me technique, noting the brevity of such experiences. Later in the chapter, you'll find a tool (Figure 3.2) for planning and using Show Me as you teach.

Responses to the questions in Figure 3.1 should help you in considering the everyday use of Show Me as, essentially, a more in-depth extension of the observation or interview. Remember that, in most cases, Show Me will be a quick request for a student or perhaps small group of students to demonstrate what they are doing within the day's mathematics lesson. That said, you could also ask your entire class to complete a Show Me activity and do a walkthrough of the responses to get a quick read of their level of success, possible mathematical challenges, or misconceptions related to the activity. You may sample students daily for Show Me opportunities or perhaps target students for Show Me based on particular needs, including as a quick assessment of the prerequisite conceptual and/or procedural knowledge necessary for the lesson of the day. Show Me is *your* opportunity to engage students in showing/demonstrating their conceptual understandings, procedural knowledge, use of particular representations or tools, and their engagement of the Standards for Mathematical Practice (NGA Center & CCSSO, 2010), particularly, but not exclusively, reasoning and modeling with mathematics.

SHOW ME

Figure 3.1 • Planning for Show Me

1. Why would you use the Show Me technique?

- As you consider the use of Show Me, what particular aspects of your lesson would be most conducive to having students show or demonstrate their understandings?
- What might you observe or expect to observe your students doing that might prompt you to use the Show Me technique?
- As you interview students in a particular lesson and consider the content and related instructional focus of the lesson, when might an interview transition to the more performance-based Show Me technique?
- Note: As you consider the importance of a full understanding of the progress of your students in mathematics, the differentiation potential of Show Me allows you to address particular student needs through the use of Show Me as well as note different responses to the same Show Me prompt.

2. Where might Show Me opportunities occur within your lesson?

- How might you use Show Me as students are working independently within the day's lesson?
- How might you use small group or whole class opportunities for students to show you how and why they completed a particular activity before releasing them to independent activities?
- Can you think of particular students or groups of students who might benefit from regular opportunities to show you how and why they completed particular elements of a lesson's activities?

3. How will you organize your classroom to implement Show Me each day?

- As you consider your implementation of the Show Me technique, how might you design a particular place in the classroom for Show Me or take advantage of the at-their-seat, in-the-moment spontaneity for implementation of Show Me?
- How might you provide easy access to representation tools as needed for a Show Me response (e.g., drawings, manipulative materials)?
- As with the interview, for particular areas of interest/concern, how might you record Show Me responses using a video or audio recording, or perhaps an interactive whiteboard app (e.g., Explain Everything™, Educreations, or ShowMe interactive whiteboards)?

4. As you implement Show Me, what entrée questions/statements might you use as you seek a deeper understanding of student thinking? Consider the following as possible examples.

- Can you show me how you did/are doing that example and explain your reasoning?
- Show me how to solve that problem using a number line (or any other related representation tool).

- Show and share your solution strategy with me.
- Show and share your solution strategy with your team member, making sure to describe how and why you did what you did.

5. What might you anticipate from students? (Consider understandings, possible mathematical challenges or misconceptions and extensions of the mathematics presented, as well as evidence of student disposition.)

- As you plan the lesson, before engaging students in the Show Me activity, reflect on your class and its progress, and anticipate the types of responses you may receive. Would the Show Me prompts used reflect conceptual or procedural understandings? Would your students be able to recount, orally or in writing, their reasoning?
- How might you consider selecting a sample of your class for Show Me each day, using the responses to monitor and advise your planning as well as identify individual student needs? The sample should be representative of the achievement range within the class, including students who may struggle, high-achieving students, and students whose achievement seems to vary from week to week or even day to day.

6. How might you follow up after a Show Me request?

- What might you ask or do as you consider a Show Me response?
- If additional Show Me follow-up is considered, would it consist of additional examples?
- How might Show Me responses influence your planning for the next day's lesson?

Tools for Using Show Me in the Classroom

As you plan the daily use of the Formative 5, it will be important to consider how the trio of assessment techniques—observations, interviews, Show Me—can be used to not only monitor your instruction but also provide you with feedback as to the relative success of your planning as well as student progress. As you think about what you will observe, and when you might interview your students, you will also consider particular opportunities for using the Show Me technique.

Consider the following classroom-based examples as merely a sampling, with actual classroom vignettes provided, of why you might ask students to show what they are doing or have done within a particular mathematics lesson:

1. **As you observe a written or hear an oral student response, use Show Me to understand what was done and why.**

SHOW ME

Classroom-Based Example: *Paige, a fifth grader, was saying to her math partner that if you just doubled the numerator and denominator of any fraction (e.g., $\frac{2}{3}$) the fraction would still be the same. What would you ask Paige to show you to indicate her understanding of her statement?*

2. **Use a sampling of Show Me requests, individual student and/or small group, to determine how students complete an activity integral to the day's lesson.**

   Classroom-Based Example: *In Laura's class, her sixth-grade students did their math seat work in groups. In today's lesson, she was having them use ratio tables to help them determine and extend the unit rate for purchasing soft drinks. As she observed her students completing this activity, Laura noted that Chase and his partner were discussing this problem, orally stating that if the unit rate was one bottle for twenty-five cents, that meant the cost for two bottles was fifty cents, four bottles was one dollar, and eight bottles was two dollars. However, they did not indicate the cost of three, five, six, or seven bottles, nor were they using the ratio table to represent their findings. Laura asked them to use the ratio table below and show her how to determine the other amounts.*

1	2	3	4	5	6	7	8
25 cents	50 cents		$1.00				$2.00

3. **Use Show Me to monitor the progress of particular students who may lack mathematics prerequisite knowledge or have missed instructional time on a topic.**

   Classroom-Based Example: *Jenni strategically used Show Me to monitor the progress of two of her fourth-grade students. Todd has missed more than a week of school due to illness. Jenni was using Show Me each day with him to help determine his progress from day to day. She found it particularly helpful to ask him to show how to divide problems like $187 \div 5$ using base ten materials. She then had him create and solve word problems to provide a context for his division examples, making sure that Todd discussed his reasoning when solving the problem. She felt that Todd was growing in his understanding of how to use the manipulative tools to represent division problems and their solution as well* *as connecting division to real-life contexts that made sense to him.*

Jenni was also concerned about Monique's progress with division and also asked her to show how she would use the base ten materials to solve $187 \div 5$. This was helpful since she noted that Monique seemed quite facile in her use of the materials to solve the problem, but seemed challenged when asked to create a word problem to show a context for this and other division situations. Jenni decided to regularly use a word problem context for all additional lessons involving division, making sure to engage her students in both representing the problem's solution and asking them to discuss their reasoning.

4. **Use Show Me to challenge. As students successfully demonstrate progress/understanding of the day's lesson focus, be prepared to use Show Me to challenge those students by extending the mathematical focus of the lesson.**

    Classroom-Based Example: *Jeff observed two of his sixth graders, Amina and Rasheed, as they were summarizing data by reporting the mean and median height of trees the school planted four years ago. He noted that all responses were correct and wanted to challenge Amina and Rasheed. He asked them to show him how they would determine the median and mean if ten additional trees, each four feet tall, were found. Jeff regularly planned for and included such extensions as possible Show Me's for his more advanced students.*

5. **Identify understandings and use a sampling of Show Me responses to advise planning for the next day's lesson and the identification of possible small group needs.**

    Classroom-Based Example: *Melissa sampled at least five students every day with a Show Me request. She then used the range of these responses to help her guide her planning for the next day with possible implications for content, pace of the next day's lesson, and use of Show Me to help define small group activities.*

6. **Be prepared with a Show Me request that would extend a student's knowledge beyond the focus of the day's lesson.**

    Classroom-Based Example: *Robert liked to use Show Me with particular students to get a glimpse of what he might do in tomorrow's lesson. Today, his third-grade students were creating their own multiplication tables using graph paper.*

Figure 3.2 • Small Group: Show Me Record

SHOW ME: Mathematics Content: *Grade 5: Number and Operations—Fractions*	
Lesson Focus/Standard: *Recognize and generate equivalent fractions. Explain why the fractions are equivalent (e.g., by using a visual fraction model).*	Anticipated Student Show Me Responses: *I wanted the students to show me how they used fraction strips to find multiple equivalent representations for* $\frac{1}{2}, \frac{1}{4}, \frac{2}{3}, \frac{3}{4}$.
Student: *Liam*  *"Look! I made four ways! These are the only ones I can see. I think there are more, but I don't know if there could be more ways to make* $\frac{1}{2}$."	**Student:** *Roberto* 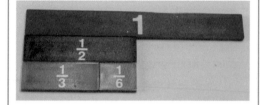 *"* $\frac{1}{3}$ *and* $\frac{1}{6}$ *equal* $\frac{1}{2}$*, but I don't get how I write it. How can we say these two fractions are equivalent or the same?"*
Student: *Marcy*  *"I found five ways to make* $\frac{1}{2}$*. I decided to organize them by size of the parts. So, I noticed something! The smaller parts mean that there are more—so like* $\frac{6}{12} = \frac{1}{2}$*. A* $\frac{1}{12}$ *is much smaller than a* $\frac{1}{4}$ *so* $\frac{2}{4} = \frac{1}{2}$*."*	**Student:** *Casey*  *"I found* $\frac{3}{6} = \frac{1}{2}$*, but then I found this other way, but I am not sure it works. I can't get this* $\frac{1}{12}$ *to line up here."*

 A blank template version of this figure is available for download at
http://resources.corwin.com/Formative5

SHOW ME

Tomorrow, he hoped to have them use the completed tables to discuss patterns, factors, and products, and perhaps begin work connecting division to multiplication. He gathered Toby, Anna, and Marisha and asked them to show him how many of their factors had 24 as the product (e.g., 3, 8; 4, 6), then asked them to explain the different ways to use the factors to determine the product 24. He was hoping they would remember the commutative property here and how the table demonstrates its use. He also asked the students how they might use the table and the product 24 to think about 24 divided by 3. Robert felt that these preplanning Show Me responses always helped him jump-start his next-day planning.

The tools and student responses to the following Show Me prompts will be helpful to you as you consider the everyday use of Show Me in your classroom. The Small Group: Show Me Record (Figure 3.2) provides a recording of Show Me responses from a sampling of students based on any of the needs/uses discussed earlier. This tool helps in organizing and providing an actual record of student responses, which you can then consider as you plan for the next day's lesson. Given the performance nature of Show Me, we have found that pictures along with a brief, accompanying notation are a quick way to document student Show Me responses. Access the tool in Figure 3.2 for your use at **http://resources.corwin.com/Formative5**. It should also be noted that this tool could easily be adapted as an individual student Show Me.

The classroom-based examples that follow both involved use of the Explain Everything™ interactive whiteboard app as a Show Me tool. The responses to particular tasks and the teacher suggestions as to how the Show Me responses were both interpreted and used for planning are included.

*   *   *

Students in Mr. Cardoza's fourth-grade class provided responses to the following problem:

> Beth's family decided to drive to Ski Round Top, which was about 680 miles from their home. Jon had a much shorter drive, which was about $\frac{1}{2}$ the distance that Beth's family drove. How much farther did Beth's family have to drive?

As Mr. Cardoza observed students, he selected Annika and Chayse to show their representations using the Explain Everything™

Annika's Work

http://resources
.corwin.com/Formative5

whiteboard app. Annika's response, involving a mental math approach, is provided in Figure 3.3. She decomposed 680 into 600 and 80, and then broke 600 into two groups of 300, and 80 into two groups of 40, arriving at 340 miles. Mr. Cardoza made note of her representation and Annika explained, "Half of the distance that Beth's family drove is Jon's amount. And Beth's family drove 680 miles, and half of that is 340 miles."

Figure 3.3 • Annika's Work

$$680 \div 2 = 340$$

300   300   40   40

340 miles

Mr. Cardoza then observed Chayse's work. Chayse had also translated the problem into dividing 680 by 2 and used the long division algorithm (see Figure 3.4). When Chayse discussed his Show Me response, it revealed his ability to decontextualize, using numbers and symbols to explain the steps in the procedure for dividing 680 by 2.

Figure 3.4 • Chayse's Initial Work

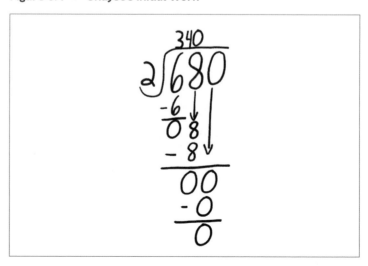

SHOW ME

Mr. Cardoza wondered if there was any evidence that Chayse could contextualize—or make sense of—the quantities and relate them to the problem involving distance. Mr. Cardoza asked Chayse if he could show his reasoning using a picture or diagram. Chayse's diagram is provided in Figure 3.5. He explained, "Okay, you have to have this house on the left . . . and [Beth's] going to Ski Round Top—say that's all the way over here [draws a horizontal line]. Jon's house would be half of that, which is right here [draws a house at the halfway point on the line]. This would be [and labels] Ski Round Top." This model could work, but does Chayse realize that Jon's house might not be directly between Beth's and Ski Round Top?

Chayse's Initial Work

http://resources
.corwin.com/Formative5

Figure 3.5 • Chayse's Show Me

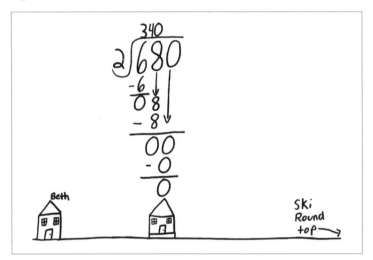

Mr. Cardoza observed other students as they worked and collected each student representation for that problem. He realized that most students solved using methods and representations similar to Annika's and Chayse's (using mental math or the long division algorithm). Mr. Cardoza reflected on the effectiveness of using a Show Me prompt with his students as a technique to help get a real sense of whether or not they can contextualize, understanding that 340 miles represents both the halfway point (got it) as well as how much farther Beth had to drive than Jon (maybe, but not completely sure). He planned to follow up with a full-class discussion involving an examination of student representations such as Annika's and Chayse's, followed by questions designed to get a sense of whether or not students understood "340 miles" as the value of how much farther away Beth's house was from Ski Round Top than Jon's.

*   *   *

Mrs. Hu's seventh graders worked on the following task:

> Cam took 15 shots and made 9 of them, scoring 18 points. He had the same shooting percentage in his next game; how many shots could Cam have made in that game?

Alanna, Jordan, and Kyra also shared their reasoning using the Explain Everything™ app. Figure 3.6 shows how Alanna divided $\frac{9}{15}$ the greatest common factor of 3, and used $\frac{3}{5}$ to generate an equivalent fraction $\left(\frac{6}{10}\right)$ to find Cam's shooting percentage (60%).

Figure 3.6 • Alanna's Work

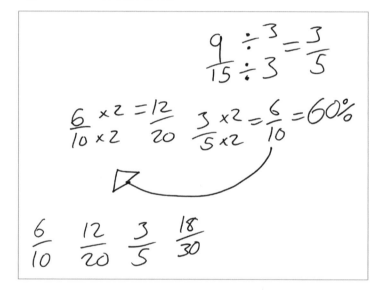

She used common factors to find other equivalent fractions and stated, "He could have gone 6 for 10, 12 for 20, 3 for 5, or 18 for 30. Basically, just anything that equaled 60%." It's worth noting that having the animated, audio version of Alanna's solution provided Mrs. Hu with a well-articulated learning artifact that helped her get a true sense of Alanna's procedural and conceptual understanding—one that could not have been gathered as easily without asking Alanna to record her Show Me using the digital app.

Mrs. Hu observed Jordan's initial solution, 60% (Figure 3.7). When asked to explain, he stated, "Nine divided by 15, that equals 60%." She agreed and asked Jordan if he could show how many shots Cam could have made using other fractions equivalent to 60%. Jordan found that $\frac{3}{5}$ and $\frac{6}{10}$ were both equivalent to 60%, and although concisely stated, he provided Mrs. Hu with evidence indicating his understanding.

Figure 3.7 • Jordan's Work

$$9 \div 15$$

$$15\overline{)9.0} \quad 60\%$$
$$\underline{-9.0}$$
$$0$$

$$\frac{9}{15} = \frac{3}{5} \qquad \frac{6}{10} = 60\%$$

$$3 \div 5 \quad 60\%$$

Kyra's approach (Figure 3.8) focused around trying to find a proportion using the cross-multiplication algorithm. She determined that Cam's shooting percentage was 60% and concluded that he "would have made 6 shots if he shot 10 times."

Kyra's Work

http://resources
.corwin.com/Formative5

SHOW ME

Figure 3.8 • Kyra's Work

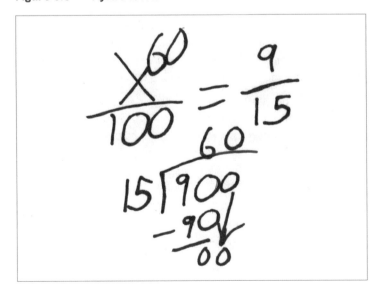

Mrs. Hu decided that a follow-up interview would be her next step with Kyra as she wanted to dig a little deeper into the meaning behind the procedure Kyra used to find Cam's shooting percentage. How were those fractions related? Why does the cross-multiplication algorithm work? Can Kyra come up with other possible solutions (the actual shots made to be equivalent to 60%)?

The Show Me responses by Mr. Cardoza's and Mrs. Hu's students demonstrate the valuable contributions such opportunities provide for impacting planning and monitoring and guiding mathematics teaching and learning.

Technology Tips and Tools for Recording Show Me Responses

There are some digital tools that provide teachers with the means to capture student Show Me responses, each of which has specific advantages. As with any digital tool that is used to collect student data, be sure to investigate and follow school district data privacy policies and practices and communicate the privacy plan and purpose of your recordings with parents/guardians and students.

1. As with other techniques, the previously mentioned interactive whiteboard apps and digital still/video recording devices and apps can be used to capture the observation of students engaged in a Show Me performance. These recordings allow teachers and students to document and review student engagement in problem solving and help inform planning for next steps.

2. A more comprehensive tool designed to improve critical thinking and communications skills, while also serving to capture and share student representations, models, and solutions is titled CueThink (http://cuethink.com). Teachers select or create their own problems, posing them to students inside the application. Students use the oft-mentioned four-step problem-solving model—Understand, Plan, Solve, Review—and have the opportunity to consider what they notice and wonder about the problem, generate an estimate, and choose an initial strategy or plan for solving the problem. Students create "thinklets" or video representations containing drawings, images, and audio using the intuitive drawing and writing tools provided within the application. Students encounter quality checks and reminders to consider as they prepare to submit their

solutions. The true power of CueThink comes into play when classmates are able to view, comment on, critique, and add annotations to one another's thinklets. These Show Me student artifacts can serve as portfolios of student reasoning and problem solving.

There are a few important considerations related to using digital tools to capture a Show Me. Careful thought should be given to the

1. Intended purpose (Is the goal to capture and archive or distribute digitally to classmates and/or the teacher?)

2. Function and ease of use of the digital tool or application (Does the tool provide an opportunity to capture information about student thinking in a way that significantly enhances what could be done without it? Can students access the tool efficiently and generate flexible representations that provide the teacher with feedback related to student understanding?)

3. Method(s) for gathering Show Me responses and providing students with feedback

   Students who have one-to-one access to devices (e.g., laptops, tablets) have a considerable advantage in terms of being able to generate and share their ideas electronically. However, a teacher with only one (or a few) digital device(s) (e.g., iPads or laptops) can, during an observation, make a Show Me request to an individual student or small group of students. The digital file can easily be saved, shared, analyzed, and discussed as a classroom learning artifact, serving as a resource to help improve learning for all students.

Using Show Me in YOUR Classroom

When planning for the use of Show Me, remember that this is a "stop-and-drop" activity where you will ask a student, pair of students, small group, or perhaps the entire class to show you how they did what they did, how a problem was solved, how a particular manipulative material or related representation was used, and so on. As the examples and Small Group: Show Me Record tool (Figure 3.3) provided in the previous section of this chapter indicated, you can use Show Me to not only validate what you have observed but also provide responses that will help in considering

Based on previous observations and interviews, you can anticipate the "lesson bumps" where Show Me might be useful.

SHOW ME

how you might redirect your instruction within the day's lesson or the planning for tomorrow's lesson.

Based on previous observations and interviews, you can anticipate the "lesson bumps" where Show Me might be useful. While it can be paired regularly with student or class observations, and serve as a prerequisite or supplement to an interview, the actual use of Show Me will be related to the content focus and student expectations of your lesson. Think about the following question: "As my students become engaged in this mathematics, what do I expect them to be able to do?" As just one example, consider having the students show how they use particular representation tools within the day's lesson (e.g., "Show me how you used the fractions bars for comparing these two fractions. What did you find out?").

Popular considerations for your use of Show Me include showing how particular procedures or representation tools are used. However, and as noted earlier in this chapter, Show Me is also useful for having students describe their reasoning and demonstrate how they solved a problem. Considering the intent and products of what's to be shown is important as you plan. Kacey, a second-/third-grade combination class teacher, noted the following:

> I use Show Me every day. One of the reasons, not the only reason, I use it is that the student responses provide me with a record of what my kids are doing. I keep copies of their work and use them during parent conferences or, as needed, for chats I might have with my principal about particular students. My Show Me responses provide me with not only a record of what my students have done, but I can actually see the growth of students within particular topics across the curriculum.

Larry, a middle school teacher, noted that he uses Show Me a lot because many of his students just need to have the lesson's focus extended to make the math a bit more challenging. He is convinced that his students have grown from providing a quick representation and short oral response to more thoughtful presentations of both solutions and the reasoning that led to the solutions. He noted that he can do this, challenge his students, without thinking he has to plan and implement an entirely different lesson to challenge them.

An important classroom consideration when using Show Me is to be prepared with regard to particular student responses. Our experience has been that, on occasion, some students could not or

SHOW ME

would not respond to Show Me or copied the responses of others. While such responses are often unexpected, think about how you might address and monitor these students (e.g., for those unwilling to respond to a Show Me request, consider having the student partner with someone and have them show their response together, or consider an interview for such students).

Finally, as you regularly consider particular components of lessons where you would want students to show what they are doing or have done, recognize the value of the performance-based documentation that Show Me provides. But also recognize how particular Show Me responses, not unlike observations, are helpful to you in guiding the pace of your lesson. A Show Me response may suggest a whole class discussion or review of a lesson topic, but it may also suggest that you quicken the pace of the day's lesson. Perhaps most importantly, Show Me responses identify areas of instructional concern in the future—for tomorrow's lesson or when you plan to teach similar concepts and skills in future years.

Summing Up

Not unlike the use of the interview, daily use of the Show Me technique extends what you observe in the classroom. As you plan, you will consider what you might observe and how such observations may become viable as interviews and Show Me's. These three techniques—observations, interviews, and Show Me—are all closely connected. They all monitor your lesson's progress and help you consider student and class readiness as you plan for tomorrow's lesson. What's more, they provide anecdotal and performance-based documentation of what your students do mathematically each day. As you plan for observing, interviewing, and Show Me, recognize that you will first monitor your students via observing as they become engaged in the day's lesson. What you observe may prompt an interview or on-the-spot use of Show Me. Your observations will dictate the frequency and flow of both the interview as well as the extent to which you use both planned or spontaneous Show Me opportunities. Together, observations, interviews, and Show Me serve as that critical filter for differentiation, which is so important to you as you plan and teach mathematics.

Professional Learning Discussion Questions

Read and discuss the following questions with your grade-level teaching team or with teams across multiple grade levels. Take notes here or use the tools in the Book Study Guide to record your thoughts.

How do you envision using a Show Me assessment in your classroom?

What challenges do you envision as you consider daily use of the Show Me technique?

Which of the Show Me examples provided in this chapter would you use or adapt for use in your classroom?

Are there particular lessons that you think would more likely engage many more Show Me opportunities than other lessons? Which? Why do you think so?

How would you describe the connection among observing, interviewing, and Show Me? How might this connection impact both your planning and your teaching?

Consider the major mathematics topics at your particular grade level. Spend time creating at least one Show Me prompt for each of these topics, making sure to find the time to share and discuss the prompts.

Notes

"I seriously think that one of the last things I got 'good' at as a teacher was questioning!"

—SIXTH- AND SEVENTH-GRADE TEACHER

"It took me a while to realize that sometimes I needed to change—while I was actually teaching— the questions that I had planned to ask."

—FOURTH-GRADE TEACHER

"The better I feel about my planning, the easier it is to frame questions and then consider responses to help me plan for the next day."

—SECOND-GRADE TEACHER

Hinge Questions: Background and Basics

Classrooms should be places where all students are expected to engage in the mathematics they are learning every day. A significant element of student engagement is found within the classroom discussions that you engineer. The ability to do this, though, is challenging. Being able to process student responses to a question, analyze the thinking expressed by your students, and then direct the next instructional steps comes with experience. But wait—what about actually asking questions, the starting point for any classroom discussion?

Teachers involve and engage their students by asking questions every day. *Principles to Actions* (NCTM, 2014) noted the importance of purposeful questions to advance reasoning and sense making, presenting a framework (Figure 4.1) of types of questions important for mathematics teaching and learning. While the question types consider levels of thinking needed for a response, each of the question types is important, depending on the intent of your lesson and the levels of understanding and engagement of your students.

Figure 4.1 • Framework for Questions Used in Mathematics Teaching

Question Type	Description
1. Gathering information	Students recall facts, justifications, or procedures.
2. Probing thinking	Students explain, elaborate, or clarify their thinking, including articulating the steps in solution methods or the completion of a task.
3. Making the mathematics visible	Students discuss mathematical structures and make connections among mathematical ideas and relationships.
4. Encouraging reflection and justification	Students reveal deeper understanding of their reasoning and actions, including making an argument for the validity of their work.

Source: Adapted from National Council of Teachers of Mathematics. (2014). *Principles to actions: Ensuring mathematics success for all.* Reston, VA: Author, pp. 36, 37. Copyright 2014, by the National Council of Teachers of Mathematics. All rights reserved.

Generally speaking, the questions you provide should be designed to provoke the mathematical reasoning of your students (NCTM, 1991). Well-posed and carefully considered questions can, and should, both elicit and extend the thinking of your students. As you well know, there are times when student responses give you a glimpse of student thinking that you had neither expected nor intended. All such responses are important and will clearly influence your planning.

There are many considerations for you as you continue to develop the craft of questioning to influence your planning and teaching as well as assess student understandings. First, plan the questions you intend to use, considering how you may need to adapt them to address particular student needs, and keeping in mind that the questions you ask are intended to engage your students by causing them to think about the mathematics they are doing. Student responses should help you determine your next instructional steps. Keep in mind that questioning is an integral component of classroom discourse. You orchestrate classroom discourse as you question, listen to student responses, ask students to clarify and justify their responses (orally or in writing), decide when and how to clarify a response, monitor students as they struggle with lesson tasks, and monitor student participation in classroom discussions. Along the way, you must provide time for students to process your questions and consider their responses, and such process time truly varies. Willingham (2009) captured this concern when he noted that "memory is the residue of thought" (p. 54). Your students will need time to process questions posed before they respond. And then, importantly, wait time comes into play. Providing a few seconds (just 3–5!) to wait for a response allows students to think through the question and provide a response that is less tentative. Yes, it's important to provide time for students to "get underneath a question" and decide how to respond. And, yes, you need to provide time to make this happen, but then what? What about the student responses? Smith and Stein (2011) describe five practices for considering and then using student responses in classroom discussions:

1. Anticipating student responses prior to the lesson

2. Monitoring students' work on and engagement with the tasks

3. Selecting particular students to present their mathematical work

4. Sequencing students' responses in a specific order for discussion

5. Connecting different students' responses and connecting the responses to key mathematical ideas

The five practices above, not unlike the Formative 5 presented in this book, provide helpful considerations as you plan for and guide classroom discussions. Note that anticipating student responses and monitoring student work directly aligns with the observation (Chapter 1), interview (Chapter 2), and Show Me (Chapter 3) formative assessment techniques, as well as the focus of this chapter—hinge questions—while the selection, sequencing, and connecting practices above focus on how you might actually engineer the discussion in your classroom.

Given the everyday importance of classroom discourse generally, and questioning in particular, linking such opportunities to formative assessment just makes sense. The work of Leahy, Lyon, Thompson, and Wiliam (2005), Wiliam (2011), and Wiliam and Leahy (2015) regarding questioning, diagnostically, at particular hinge points within a lesson allows the teacher to make instructional decisions that impact the pace and instructional sequence of a lesson. The **hinge question** provides a check for understanding or proficiency at a particular hinge point in a lesson. Stated differently, the success of a lesson actually hinges on responses to such questions as an indication of whether students understand enough to move on. Hinge question responses directly in*form* both planning and instruction. Your quick analysis of hinge question responses provides you with in-the-moment signals to guide, monitor, and shift lesson activities as you teach.

> A hinge question provides a check for understanding or proficiency at a particular hinge point in a lesson. The success of the lesson hinges on responses to such questions as an indication of whether students understand enough to move on.

Planning for Using Hinge Questions

The hinge question is the question that you ask that truly provides feedback to guide your next steps, both within your lesson, moving forward, and as you plan for the next day. The hinge question typically occurs toward the end of a lesson, but you could ask hinge point questions at particular points within a lesson where you need to get a sense of what students know before moving forward with the lesson. Consider TJ's example:

> When I have lessons where I finish one concept or skill and move on to another topic, I always use a hinge point question. The responses give me a sense of closure for one topic as I move on to the next aspect of my lesson.

HINGE QUESTIONS

Think of the following connection between the interview and hinge question formative assessment techniques. The hinge question can be thought of as a whole class or small group interview, in that the question is diagnostic in focus. Responses indicate what the class or student group knows at that point within the lesson of the day. The hinge question should assess an important element of your lesson, one of those troublesome bumps on your instructional pathway, where student responses will help you to define and map your instructional next step or steps. Ideally, your students will respond within one minute and you will analyze and interpret responses within fifteen seconds (Wiliam, 2011). In our work, we consider a two-minute hinge point window to include posing the question, obtaining student responses, and your analysis of the responses.

Like observations, interviews, and Show Me, the hinge question is integral to the planning of a lesson and deciding what is important, both mathematically and pedagogically. Our sense is that the hinge question is that make-or-break or "deal-breaker" query that helps you determine your in-the-moment instructional maneuvers and also advises your planning for the next day.

Consider the following different uses and types of hinge questions, one example at the second-grade level and the other with fifth-grade students.

> Our school faculty has been working most of the year on what our school calls the Formative 5. We meet each Friday to do a check-in on how we have been using the palette of formative assessment techniques and share what we are learning, how we are using the techniques, and how our students are doing. I had been really struggling with getting the most out of the hinge question with my second graders. I decided for my lesson, which began with place value and estimation involving three-digit whole numbers and then moved to checking for fluency with addition and subtraction within 100, that given the lesson's two areas of content focus, it just made sense to use two hinge point questions. After some whole group work, I used the following:

The Reynaldos were traveling and drove 180 miles on Monday, then over 200 miles on Tuesday and 350 miles on Wednesday. On which day did they travel the farthest? How do you know?

HINGE QUESTIONS

I had the class use manipulatives or drawings, if needed. I did a quick sharing of responses. I was pleased, then I moved on to the second stage of my lesson, which was mostly review. Toward the end of the lesson, I used the following hinge point question to decide just how the students were doing with regard to fluently adding or subtracting within 100.

Every day, Burr's dad drives 45 miles to the metro stop to get to work and then again to come back home. How many miles does he drive each day? Does he drive more or less than 100 miles every day? How do you know?

Like the lesson's first hinge point question, I had my class use manipulatives or drawings as needed to show what they did. They recorded their answers on their small dry-erase boards so it was easy for me to just spot the student answers AND their work. This worked pretty well, and although I could see their answers for how many miles Burr's dad drove each day, I ended up calling on a few students for the 'how do you know' part of the problem. A couple of things. Overall, I was pleased with the responses, and tomorrow we can move into adding columns of numbers and place value to 1,000. Also, I have become a fan of deciding who I will call on with my questions rather than the predictable hands that are always raised or not! Now I get a better sense of what a full range of my students know and can do. But the major point here is that I liked using two hinge point questions, one to assess student progress with the first part of my lesson and the other to serve as my decision maker regarding, in this case, fluency, but within a problem context. Both impacted my work with students today and my planning for tomorrow. 🙶

Zach and Kiara, both fifth-grade teachers, approached their use of the hinge question differently. Here's what Zach had to say.

🙶 Both of our classes were working on the following standard: interpret division of a whole number by a unit fraction, and compute such quotients. Kiara and I decided we would both do hinge questions toward the end of the lesson. We have learned that a hinge question close to the end of the day's lesson makes sense. When we started, we used our questions too close to the end of the lesson and we never had time to do in-the-moment instructional supports we could have implemented. Now we leave a little time so we can adapt our lesson a bit as needed, assign a particular activity, review something, have a brief discussion, and so on. Both hinge questions were based on the following problem.

Our class was laying out the 3-mile run/walk on the trail near our school. We had the students put up markers for each $\frac{1}{2}$ mile of the course. How many markers were needed?

I used a multiple-choice format for my class, and Kiara just used the question with an added phrase. Here's what our hinge questions looked like:

Zach's class:

Our class was laying out the 3-mile run/walk on the trail near our school. We had the students put up markers for each $\frac{1}{2}$ mile of the course. How many markers were needed?

A. $\frac{3}{2}$

B. $1\frac{1}{2}$

C. $\frac{1}{6}$

D. 6

Kiara's class:

Our class was laying out the 3-mile run/walk on the trail near our school. We had the students put up markers for each $\frac{1}{2}$ mile of the course. How many markers were needed? Be prepared to tell me how you know.

Here's the difference in the two approaches. My multiple-choice example took a bit more time to create because I needed to provide the answer choices, and they needed to be choices where I could tell what the students might be doing when they selected them. For example, if someone selected A or $\frac{3}{2}$, I was pretty sure they multiplied the $3 \times \frac{1}{2}$. If they selected B, they most likely added $\frac{1}{2}$ three times. For each of the choices A–D, I tried to provide a response that wasn't just random, but one that students might actually consider or do. This is the diagnostic feature of the multiple-choice format, which I like a lot. I had my students respond by just raising cards—A, B, C, or D—that I provided. This was quick, allowed me to quickly identify error types, and I had some time to then really discuss the problem and consider my next steps. Kiara's response was provided orally by the students. She said what was most revealing to her were the 'tell me how you know' responses. She sampled about six or seven responses and had most provide the correct answer. She then circulated the room and found that some either added or subtracted the 3 and the $\frac{1}{2}$, while a couple students multiplied $3 \times \frac{1}{2}$. Like me, she had time to do some more with these types of problems before math class ended.

I think Kiara and I both agree that there are advantages to both types of hinge questions. Actually creating the answer choices takes some time in the planning of the question, but certainly saves time in receiving and analyzing responses. On the other hand, the actual question without answer choices allows the teacher to get at what the students were thinking when they answered the question. We'll both continue to work on hinge questions. One thing for sure—we both realize their use guides what we will do with the time remaining in our mathematics class as well as our planning for the next day.

The uses of the hinge question discussed above indicate the level of planning needed to both craft and implement the question. Also note that depending on the focus of the lesson, hinge point questions might be used to determine particular points of progress within elements of a lesson. Our experience has been that the multiple-choice version of the hinge question is probably used more frequently in Grades 3 and up, and that many teachers like this format as it also serves as practice for seeing and responding to multiple-choice items on end-of-year summative assessments. That said, responses to a hinge question

Figure 4.2 • Planning for Hinge Questions

1. How will you use hinge questions as you teach?

- When might you use the multiple-choice format for your hinge question?
- When might you use a more typical question format for your hinge question?
- When might you consider using hinge questions at particular hinge points within a lesson?

2. If you think of the hinge question as a whole class interview, how will you use the responses?

- When using a hinge question, how will you determine whether your class is ready to move on to the next topic/lesson/standard?
- How will hinge question responses influence your on-the-spot, minute-by-minute instructional decision making?

3. How will you consider student responses to a hinge question?

- Will students use student response tools (e.g., cards, sticks, devices) when responding to your hinge questions? If so, explain how they will do so.
- How will you sample student responses to your hinge question?
- How will you ensure that you can efficiently analyze hinge question responses?

4. How will you consider types of questions for your hinge question?

- Think about how you will consider question types: gathering information, probing thinking, making the mathematics visible, or encouraging reflection and justification when you plan and compose a hinge question. How will the mathematics focus of the day determine the type of hinge question you may ask?

5. When you prepare to ask a hinge question, what might you anticipate?

- Have you carefully prepared and thought through possible responses to your hinge question?
- Should you ask the hinge question to small groups of students or the whole class?
- Should students have access to manipulative materials, dry erase boards, or devices for their response to the hinge question?

addressing a lesson hot spot, however framed, immediately identify what you will be doing next—within your remaining math time or in tomorrow's lesson. The questions and accompanying statements in Figure 4.2 should be helpful to you as you consider the use of hinge questions in your own classroom. Actual tools for considering and using hinge questions and classroom-based examples are provided in the next section of this chapter.

As noted, consideration of the statements and questions in Figure 4.2 should be helpful to you as you plan for everyday use of hinge questions both at particular hinge points within a lesson or toward the end of a lesson, depending on the content focus of your mathematics lesson of the day. It's important to remember that the hinge question is diagnostic in that responses should immediately provide an assessment of what your students know about a particular topic. Like the other formative assessment techniques, the hinge question will be integral to your lesson planning, and responses to your hinge question will determine your next steps—both in planning and instructionally. The hinge question uses what you do every day with students, which is asking questions and guiding discussion, and directs a particular question to those "I wonder if they are getting this" challenges you think about as you teach. These responses will let you know!

Tools for Using Hinge Questions in the Classroom

As you think about the use of hinge questions in your classroom, reflect on the use of observations, interviews, and the Show Me techniques, and consider their connections to the hinge question. As you observe each day, what you observe sharpens your thinking related to *when* you might ask and *what* you might ask within a hinge question, with what you observe during a lesson having the potential to suggest a revision to a hinge point or end-of-lesson hinge question you have already planned. As noted, the hinge question is, to an extent, a full class or group interview, so the interviews you might plan for and implement, and the student responses to your interview questions, may also impact the planning and use of your hinge question. Consider Barb and Heather's very different uses of the Show Me technique and how they connected it to their hinge question.

> For my hinge question, I asked my fourth graders if the difference between 45,675, and 44,702 was greater or less than 1,000? And, to be able to tell me how they knew. I had them use < or > cards I prepared. When I asked for the response, most did well, but then I decided to use Show Me and changed the 'tell me about it' part of my hinge to 'show me.' I had them use their dry erase boards for their response—some subtracted the numbers and some wrote a response. I like it that I can interchange the Formative 5 throughout my lessons.

—BARB

> For my Show Me for today's lesson, I worked with a small group of my fourth graders asking them to show me how they would determine the product of 19 × 9. Most just used the partial products algorithm, some the standard algorithm, and some used area models (e.g., a [10 + 9] × 9 grid). Then when I decided to use a hinge point question for the whole class, I asked: if you planted a garden that had 18 rows of plants with 9 plants in each row, would there be more or less than 180 plants planted? I had my students raise their < or > card to signify their response. It was easy to spot how my students responded. I like the potential of using Show Me responses to help guide my hinge questions. For today, I had the information I needed, when I needed it, at that hinge point and then moved on.

—HEATHER

Now let's move more directly to using the hinge question by considering the following questions, which are followed by classroom-based responses, and tools for hinge question use.

1. **Do I use the hinge question toward the end of every lesson, or can I use it whenever I like?**

   Classroom-Based Response: *I typically use the hinge question toward the end of my math lesson, but I make sure there is time for me to quickly ask the question and review responses (about two minutes total). Then if I need to use Show Me or just spend time reviewing a particular response or type of response from the hinge question, I have time to do so. Just last week, I asked my third-grade students whether they thought a school day lasted more or less than 10 hours, and many of them thought they were in school more than 10 hours a day. Not sure why so many responded that way, but I had time to "fix" things just by reviewing with the class when school started—8:00 a.m.— and when it ended—3:00 p.m.—and then asking the hinge question again—suggesting that, if they wanted, they could use drawings, manipulative clocks, or just consider our wall clock. Maybe they just needed time to think about my hinge question more carefully, since they sure got it on the second round! This is the main reason I provide some time not just to ask and analyze the hinge question I use, but also for next steps.*

2. **What's the difference between a hinge point question and a hinge question?**

   Classroom-Based Response: *In my classroom, the hinge question is my daily decision maker—lesson-wise. The* *responses to the hinge question help me determine what I need to plan for tomorrow's lesson and provide me with a quick sense of what students know—it's diagnostic and opens up the potential for use of the interview and Show Me techniques. The hinge point question is just a hinge question that I might use at particular points in the lesson. For example, last week we were working on perimeter and also reviewing prior work with addition and subtraction in the same lesson. So, it was perfect for two hinge point questions, one toward the end of my review work with addition and subtraction. I used this question, "Sandra took flights totaling about 3,500 miles in April and about 2,700 miles in May. How many miles did she travel, and how many more miles did she travel in April than May?" Then toward the end of the lesson, I asked the following hinge point question related to our work with perimeter. "Can you create a triangle that has a perimeter of 25 cm? Make a drawing to show your triangle and the length of each of the sides on your whiteboards." In both cases, I needed to make sure there was time to consider responses to the questions, and consider my next steps instructionally, during the time I had left within math class and for my planning for tomorrow.*

3. **Should I use a multiple-choice format hinge question or just a question?**

   Classroom-Based Response: *As a district-based and former school-based math leader, I used to wonder about this. At the primary level, particularly Grades K, 1, and 2, I sort of figured that the kids couldn't handle multiple-choice responses and weren't taking end-of-year tests using that format, so I just thought, what's the point of that? And then one day at a school meeting specifically discussing hinge questions, where I made my pronouncement, Katie took me to task a bit. She said, "You know, in second grade, every student has response cards, so we can do that. I actually do things like this all the time. I ask a question using a PowerPoint slide and then flash clues, and the students can raise their T card if true and their F card if false. For example, I can ask, 'What can you say about 27?' and then flash the following multiple-choice responses one at a time, asking them to raise their T card if true and F card if false.*

   A. *It's almost 50.*

   B. *It's > 20.*

C. It's < 30.

D. It's 1 more than 26.

Sometimes I add 'E. What else?' as a choice. When I do, I always get some interesting responses, but then the hinge takes a bit longer, more than the two minutes I like to use for what we call 'hinge time.'" While I love Katie's idea and it certainly works, I still think the multiple-choice type hinge question is more for Grades 3–up. However, I do know it takes less time for teachers to pose multiple-choice format hinge questions; receive responses (electronically, using every student respond devices, raising hands, or completing a paper-pencil version of the question); and analyze them, rather than moving around the classroom and spot-checking written responses. The time demand for the multiple-choice hinge question is on the front end, actually planning the question, and considering the answer choices for a carefully designed multiple-choice hinge question. So should you prefer a focused question and a quick review of responses by several students to the multiple-choice formatted hinge question? My experience has shown that, to an extent, the mathematics focus of the lesson, your background and comfort with questioning, and time all play into this decision. The major point is that the hinge question guides your in-the-classroom, in-the-moment next steps and influences your planning that afternoon or evening, as the next question discusses.

4. **How and when do I plan for the hinge question?**

Classroom-Based Response: *Each night when I plan for mathematics, my planning includes what I will anticipate observation-wise, elements of my lesson that would cause me to interview students or use Show Me, and when and how I will use the hinge question for that or those trouble bumps in my lesson, where I just need to know what my kids know. I found the Planning: Hinge Question Considerations Tool (Figure 4.3) to be particularly helpful to me when I first began using hinge questions. It really helped me think about whether my hinge question would be appropriate. Since then, I have "graduated" into everyday use of the Classroom: Hinge Question Implementation Tool (Figure 4.4). It's now my go-to resource.*

Figure 4.3 • Planning: Hinge Question Considerations Tool

Date: April 7		
Hinge Question: There was $\frac{1}{2}$ of the pie left. It was shared by 3 people. How much of a pie did each person have? Show how you know using a drawing.		
	Yes	**No**
Will the hinge question assess important mathematical understandings of the day?	X	
Will students understand the question?	X	
Will students be able to respond in about a minute?	X	
Will expected responses be such that they can be analyzed and interpreted quickly?	X	

General Consideration: Will responses assist in shaping planning for tomorrow's lesson?

Circle one: (Yes)   No   (If no, revise hinge question)

Yes, and I may use responses to frame an exit task for tomorrow's lesson or have the students create exit tasks we can try out on the class.

How?
We have just begun our work with multiplication and division of fractions, working mostly using representations, so I want to see how they know that if 3 share, they each get $\frac{1}{3}$ of the pie, so $\frac{1}{3}$ of $\frac{1}{2}$ pie is $\frac{1}{6}$ using a drawing. Their drawings should represent $\frac{1}{6}$ of a pie for each of the 3 people sharing the pie.

Source: Fennell, F., Kobett, B., & Wray, J. (2015). Classroom-based formative assessments: Guiding teaching and learning. In C. Suurtamm (Ed.) & A. McDuffie (Series Ed.), *Annual perspectives in mathematics education: Assessment to enhance teaching and learning* (pp. 51–62). Reston, VA: National Council of Teachers of Mathematics. Republished with permission of the National Council of Teachers of Mathematics; permission conveyed through Copyright Clearance Center, Inc.

 A blank template version of this figure is available for download at **http://resources.corwin.com/Formative5**

The Planning: Hinge Question Considerations Tool (Figure 4.3), as noted above, is helpful in early efforts as you consider everyday use of the hinge question, guiding your decision making as you plan for the use of the hinge question. This tool helps you in actually planning for and framing the hinge question. Once you feel more comfortable with the considerations for any hinge question—multiple-choice format or question-and-response format—the

Figure 4.4 • Classroom: Hinge Question Implementation Tool

Date: April 15	

Mathematics Standard: Grade 7: Expressions and Equations—Solve word problems leading to equations of the form $ax + b = c$ and $a(x + b) = c$, where a, b, and c are specific rational numbers.

Hinge Question: The perimeter of an isosceles triangle is 72 cm. If one side is 12 cm, what is the length of each of the two equal sides? Response choices:

A. 24, since $3 \times 24 = 72$ cm

B. 60, since $60 + 12 = 72$ cm

C. 30, since $(2 \times 30) + 12 = 72$ cm

D. 42, since $2 \times 42 - 12 = 72$ cm

Location in the Lesson	Anticipated Student Responses	Possible Next Steps: Differentiation Strategy
Beginning	Anticipate that most will recognize the two equal sides with each side being 30 cm. Some concern that they will not remember/know to respond based on each of the two equal sides; or that some will continue to think rectangles, not triangles. We have worked with/on rectangles all week.	**Review** Consider reviewing names of triangle types, which may be getting in the way of the standard being addressed in the lesson.
Middle		**Extend** • Use other examples beyond measurement geometry. • Request equations or expressions within the response (as appropriate).
End Will use this toward the end of the lesson—multiple-choice format		**Student Grouping** Might consider Show Me or an interview based on responses.

 A blank template version of this figure is available for download at
http://resources.corwin.com/Formative5

Classroom: Hinge Question Implementation Tool (see Figure 4.4) will become an element of your lesson planning. It's most frequently used as teachers actually implement the hinge question. Download these tools for your own use and adaptation at **http://resources .corwin.com/Formative5**. It should also be noted that this tool could easily be adapted as an individual student Show Me.

As you plan and become acquainted with use of the hinge question, note that we have also found it helpful to actually try out hinge questions with colleagues within a grade-level community of learning. Such trial opportunities will also provide you with occasions to both discuss and consider the use of a multiple-choice and question-like hinge question format as well as discuss lessons where particular hinge point questions within a lesson, rather than one hinge question, would make sense.

The two examples that follow, one at the primary grade level and one for middle school students, demonstrate actual use of hinge questions. What's most important is how the teachers were able to quickly analyze and make the diagnostic decisions that use of the hinge question affords.

Grade 1—Addition and Subtraction: Hannah asked her first-grade students to use their individual dry-erase boards to respond to the following hinge question toward the end of her math lesson:

> Bryce has 17 stamps from the United States and Canada. If 6 are from Canada, how many are from the United States?

While she had already planned the content (use addition and subtraction within twenty to solve word problems involving addition and subtraction situations) of her small group instructional rotations for math, she wanted to make sure that her students were placed correctly. She designed the hinge question to ensure accurate placement of the students. She has noticed that the student responses to the hinge question often surprise her, and it was critical for her to use this "in time" information to decide the next instructional steps for tomorrow.

Hannah anticipated that many of her students would draw a representation for all of the stamps and use some sort of take from or crossing-out strategy to determine the remaining stamps. She also believed that another group of students would use computation to solve the problem. Her plan was to divide the students into two groups to continue to work on unpacking take from and compare word problem situations.

As she looked across her classroom at the students' whiteboards, she noted the following responses (Figure 4.5).

Figure 4.5 • Grade 1 Student Work

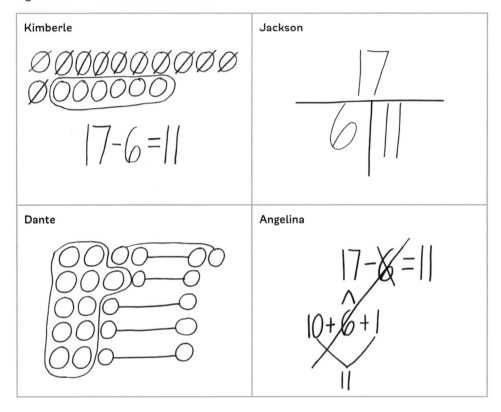

Generally, students responded as Hannah anticipated. Kimberle loved to draw everything to represent her thinking and always seemed to use a cross-out strategy for subtraction. She was glad that Kimberle seemed to have some conceptual understanding, but really wanted to see if she can get her to use some flexible strategies.

Hannah was thrilled that Jackson used the part/part/whole organizer to show his thinking. She thought he might draw circles and was pleased that he was able to see how this problem fit into the part/part/whole.

Hannah was very surprised by two students' responses. As she looked over Dante's response, she noticed that he was using a compare strategy to subtract. Conceptually, this is important understanding for students, and she is always interested when students record their thinking in this way. She anticipated that Dante would record his thinking with a number sentence and was perplexed that he decided to make a drawing.

Angelina's response was the most surprising. Just last week, Angelina was drawing circles and crossing out items to represent subtraction. Hannah was thrilled to see her decompose to subtract and decided to use her response to begin the small group instruction discussion.

Once again, Hannah was thrilled to use the hinge technique to guide her instructional grouping. Without this important information, she would have placed students incorrectly. Now, she was ready to target the students' instructional needs with purpose and clarity. While this question and the drawing and Hannah's analysis extended beyond her 2-minute rule for the hinge question, it was worth it and she was able to spot responses by this rotation and do her analysis in less than three minutes.

Grade 7—Adding and Subtracting Rational Numbers: Melena and her seventh-grade class were studying properties of operations as strategies to add and subtract rational numbers (7.NS.A.1.D). Today's lesson involved the addition and subtraction of integers. A challenge Melena had been facing in her teaching was how she could seamlessly pose a hinge question, allow students to respond in a timely fashion, and then analyze and interpret the results efficiently. She learned about a digital tool called "Formative" (http://goformative.com) where teachers create/select multiple-choice, short answer, true/false, or show me questions. This tool allows students quick access from any digital device, where they can generate solutions using a digital whiteboard interface. Formative is free, so Melena decided to try it in the beginning of her class one day. She added the following hinge question and sent students the direct link, allowing them to use classroom laptops or their own devices:

> What was the temperature at the end of the day? Samantha was in charge of recording the morning and afternoon temperature for her class. This morning it was really cold. Samantha recorded the temperature as −7° F. The temperature rose 15° F when Samantha had to record the temperature at noon. And then the temperature dropped 6° F when she had to record the temperature at the end of the day. Use a vertical number line to represent the temperature changes and write an equation to represent the changes and temperature at the end of the day.

Melena was very interested to see if students could apply their understanding of addition and subtraction of integers to solve a problem involving rising/falling temperature readings. Would they be able to represent the situation using both a vertical number line and an equation?

Shortly after students began working, Melena was able to monitor their work in real time using the screen shown in Figure 4.6.

She was able to analyze their work quickly and found that most students were able to represent the solution correctly using a vertical number line and an equation. However, upon quick visual analysis, Min's and Rachel's responses included errors, possibly related to interpreting the positive/negative values of certain temperatures, which translated into errors in the vertical number line representations and equations. Melena decided to use the hinge question results to continue with instruction on this topic. She selected Min, Joseph, Dan, and Michelle to share their reasoning, allowing them to go up to her computer, select their work, and share with the whole class. Not surprisingly, both Min and Rachel corrected their own mistakes based on comments and questions from their peers. Melena decided to let them both resubmit their

Figure 4.6 • "Recording Temperatures" Hinge Question Using "Formative" Tool (http://goformative.com)

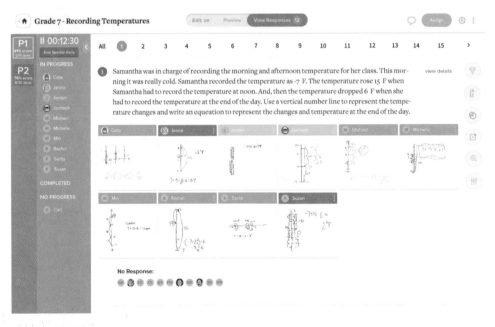

Source: Courtesy of goformative.com.

work. At one point during the whole class discussion, Sarita, who created a horizontal number line, revealed that she had never used a vertical number line before (Who knew?). A classmate reminded Joseph that he should write an equation to represent the change in the day's temperature.

Melena reflected that in this case, having the digital student learning artifacts available for the entire class to view provided students with the opportunity to address mistakes or bumps in reasoning, minimizing her role in the process. She also considered that one of the best features of Formative was that it provided a live visual of student responses in action while in the teacher's view, thus allowing her to use the hinge question responses for in-the-moment teaching!

Technology Tips and Tools for Recording Hinge Questions

There are several online tools that can be used to pose hinge questions and then quickly collect and review student responses. As with all technology tools, be sure that any online applications are approved for use by your school/district and are used in line with existing policies. All of the following tools are designed to respect the privacy of users and are available to use free of charge.

- **Google Forms** (http://www.google.com/forms): Teachers can develop hinge questions that allow for many response formats (e.g., multiple choice, check all that apply, short answer, extended response, rating scale). Students can use any web-enabled device to read, respond, and even edit their responses (if permitted by the teacher). The teacher is able to view individual student responses and a summary of student data, analyze data in a spreadsheet, and/or download the spreadsheet.

- **Kahoot** (http://getkahoot.com): Students log in on any web-enabled device with a pin code to respond to a question or questions posed by the teacher. Students receive immediate feedback on whether they are correct or incorrect. A competitive aspect of Kahoot ranks students on a leader scoreboard based on their accuracy and response speed.

- **Padlet** (https://padlet.com): Padlet is an open space where teachers can pose a question and allow users an opportunity to tap or click on the screen and quickly type

HINGE QUESTIONS

a response and even add audio, video, still image, and document attachment files. After responses have been submitted, the teacher can choose to view the responses in a grid format, which is helpful for quickly assessing student thinking.

- **Plickers** (https://plickers.com)**:** Teachers install the free app and print out the free QR code cards (https://plickers.com/cards). When setting up a class, each student is assigned a card with a unique number. Each side of the shape on the card corresponds with a different answer choice (A, B, C, D). After the teacher poses a multiple-choice or true/false question, the students hold up their response cards. The teacher scans the room using the app, which records each student response and displays and archives the data.

- **TodaysMeet** (http://todaysmeet.com)**:** Originally designed to capture backchannel conversations, TodaysMeet enables teachers to pose questions and collect typed responses (limited to 140 characters or less) quickly. Everything is displayed in real time, and teachers can save a transcript for postanalysis.

Remember that a key to posing hinge questions and assessing student responses includes time-efficient practices. Be sure you test them on different devices (handheld, tablets, laptops, desktop computers) and browsers ahead of time to ensure that their use to support hinge questions is seamless and effective.

Using Hinge Questions in YOUR Classroom

As noted, the drafting of hinge questions occurs during the planning of a lesson. Creating and implementing the hinge question will help you in your planning and teaching, as the hinge question will focus on an important component of your lesson. The hinge question should address one of those important instructional hurdles of your lesson. And, if your lesson addresses multiple concepts, skills, or mathematical connections, you may elect to plan for hinge point questions at the appropriate content breaks within such a lesson. Your experience in the classroom will help you as you anticipate student responses to your hinge questions, as well as potential next steps within the lesson or the next day.

Your everyday experience with observations, interviews, and Show Me will actually influence and help you as you prepare for using the hinge question. Consider the following comments from Zak:

> Of course I use a hinge question every day. It has become part of my lesson planning routine. First, I look at where I am going tomorrow math-wise, and then decide if it would be better to do hinge point questions at particular content breaks in my lesson or just use the hinge question toward the end of the lesson. I usually present the hinge question with about fifteen to twenty minutes left in my mathematics time. This is my 'time cushion' for in-the-moment next steps based on student responses to my hinge. It also allows me to finish up with the hinge and gives my students enough time to get started with their exit task (Chapter 5). I like the multiple-choice format of the hinge question, but only use that about two to three days most weeks—that's just me. These take me a little longer to create, so I have to figure that time into my planning. My team and I have created a file of all of our hinge questions, so we now go to the file and can reuse or adapt them to our needs. Late at night, when I am planning, it is so nice to be able to go to our hinge files and either use or adapt a question for my use. Sometimes I turn a regular hinge question into a multiple-choice hinge question. When I take a final look at my plans for tomorrow, I try to anticipate responses to my hinge or hinge point questions, particularly considering how I will monitor responses—every pupil response, circulating the class, or just sampling student responses. I know my kids, and this planning helps me think about the math bumps some of them have—and that's how I determine the hinge questions.

The planning and classroom implementation tools (Figures 4.3 and 4.4) presented in the previous section of the chapter should be helpful to you as you think about, plan for, and actually use hinge questions in your classroom. A number of comments may come to mind as you're doing this. As stated, responses to your hinge question are the lesson's "deal-breaker." How are my students doing? What are my next steps? Responses to your hinge question provide the class pulse you need to have as you consider the pace of your instruction. OK to move on? Do they need more time on a topic? Do I need to interview some students? And finally, the hinge question, together with the other techniques presented in this book, all become the assessment palette that guides your mathematics planning and instruction and, importantly, provides a comprehensive and living portfolio of the mathematical progress of your students.

Summing Up

The hinge question extends the Formative 5 to include a technique that becomes, to an extent, a diagnostic extension of the interview for a whole class. The hinge question is an important element of every lesson. Responses to the hinge question and their analysis essentially identify the starting line for the immediate adjustment of the day's lesson, if needed, and for guiding the planning of the next day's lesson. The hinge question may be used toward the end of your mathematics lesson or at particular hinge points within your lesson, depending on the mathematics content focus of your day. The hinge question may be framed and presented as a question and presented orally or in writing or as a multiple-choice formatted question. Ideally, students will respond within 1 minute and you will analyze and interpret responses within 15 seconds (Wiliam, 2011). Our sense is that, optimally, use of the hinge question, student responses, and your analysis takes about two minutes. The hinge question captures a truly important element of the day's lesson and is a key element to your planning and teaching every single day.

Notes

Professional Learning Discussion Questions

Read and discuss the following questions with your grade-level teaching team or with teams across multiple grade levels. Take notes here or use the tools in the Book Study Guide to record your thoughts.

How will you consider creating hinge questions as you plan your mathematics lessons?

What every-student-response techniques or materials might your students use as they respond to hinge questions?

Are there particular content topics that may be more appropriate for the multiple-choice format of the hinge question than others?

How can you use observations, interviews, and the Show Me technique to assist in your use of the hinge question?

How might your learning community plan for and develop hinge questions?

How might your learning community share, discuss, and reflect on student responses to hinge questions? How might it adapt them for future use?

The hinge question is considered to be diagnostic, as discussed in the chapter. How does the hinge question differ from other questions you may ask of your students?

How might you plan for a range of hinge questions that might be used across grade-level teams?

Notes

_____

_____

_____

_____

_____

_____

_____

_____

"It really has taken me a while to move beyond what we used to do for an exit ticket to using an exit task. My tickets were trivial—just quick, mostly routine math computation. Now, my tasks focus on problem solving and reasoning."

—THIRD-GRADE TEACHER

"I admit to struggling when trying, particularly at the end of a long day, to create exit tasks. I now have great sources which I use regularly to jump-start my thinking as I create or adapt previously used tasks. How my students do on their exit tasks is very important to me. Their progress helps define my next steps."

—SIXTH-GRADE TEACHER

CHAPTER 5
EXIT TASKS

Exit Tasks: Background and Basics

"Effective formative assessment involves using tasks that elicit evidence of students' learning, then using that evidence to inform subsequent instruction" (NCTM, 2014, p. 95). This chapter presents the exit task, our final classroom-based formative assessment technique. We consider exit tasks as end-of-the-lesson formative assessments. Note that the emphasis here, particularly language-wise, is on an exit task rather than the more commonly used exit ticket (or slip). The intent of the entry (or exit) ticket (or slip) strategy (Fisher & Frey, 2004) is to help students summarize and reflect on their learning.

The **exit task** is a capstone problem or task that captures the major focus of the lesson for that day or perhaps the past several days and provides a sampling of student performance. For many, locating or creating the mathematical task to be used as the exit task is a challenge. In fact, it's a multifaceted challenge. Not all tasks provide the same level of opportunity for student thinking and learning (Hiebert et al., 1997; Stein, Smith, Henningsen, & Silver, 2009). We know that mathematical activities can range from an exercise or set of exercises to a complex problem or task that involves much higher cognitive demand. Consider the two examples below:

> The **exit task** is a capstone problem or task that captures the major focus of the lesson and provides a sampling of student performance.

Exercise	High Cognitive Task
$2\frac{1}{2} \div 4 =$	Use a drawing or manipulatives to represent the solution to the following problem: There were $2\frac{1}{2}$ pies left from the party. If 4 people shared the leftover pies, how much pie would each person receive? What if 5 people shared the leftover pie? How much pie for each person?

Smith and Stein (1998) have developed a mathematics task analysis guide (Figure 5.1) that provides characteristics of low-level and high-level tasks and can be used to analyze tasks that you may select or create for use as exit tasks.

Figure 5.1 • Mathematics Task Analysis Guide

Levels of Demands

Lower-Level Demands (Memorization)

- Involve either reproducing previously learned facts, rules, formulas, or definitions or committing facts, rules, formulas, or definitions to memory
- Cannot be solved using procedures because a procedure does not exist or because the time frame in which the task is being completed is too short to use a procedure
- Are not ambiguous. Such tasks involve the exact reproduction of previously seen material, and what is the best reproduced is clearly and directly stated.
- Have no connection to the concepts or meaning that underlie the facts, rules, formulas, or definitions being learned or reproduced

Lower-Level Demands (Procedures Without Connections)

- Are algorithmic. Use of the procedure either is specifically called for or is evident from prior instruction, experience, or placement of the task.
- Require limited cognitive demand for successful completion. Little ambiguity exists about what needs to be done and how to do it.
- Have no connection to the concepts or meaning that underlie the procedure being used
- Are focused on producing correct answers instead of on developing mathematical understanding
- Require no explanations or explanations that focus solely on describing the procedure that was used

High-Level Demands (Procedures With Connections)

- Focus students' attention on the use of procedures for the purpose of developing deeper levels of understanding of mathematical concepts and ideas
- Suggest explicitly or implicitly pathways to follow that are broad general procedures that have close connections to underlying conceptual ideas as opposed to narrow algorithms that are opaque with respect to underlying concepts
- Usually are represented in multiple ways, such as visual diagrams, manipulatives, symbols, and problem situations. Making connections among multiple representations helps develop meaning.
- Require some degree of cognitive effort. Although general procedures may be followed, they cannot be followed mindlessly. Students need to engage in conceptual ideas that underlie the procedures to complete the task successfully and that develop understanding.

Higher-Level Demands (Doing Mathematics)

- Require complex and nonalgorithmic thinking—a predictable, well-rehearsed approach or pathway is not explicitly suggested by the task, task instructions, or a worked-out example
- Require students to explore and understand the nature of mathematical concepts, processes, or relationships
- Demand self-monitoring or self-regulation of one's own cognitive processes
- Require students to access relevant knowledge and experiences and make appropriate use of them in working through the task
- Require students to analyze the task and actively examine task constraints that may limit possible solution strategies and solutions
- Require considerable cognitive effort and may involve some level of anxiety for the student because of the unpredictable nature of the solution process required

Source: These characteristics are derived from the work of Doyle on academic tasks (1988) and Resnick on high-level-thinking skills (1987), the *Professional Standards for Teaching Mathematics* (NCTM, 1991), and the examination and categorization of hundreds of tasks used in QUASAR classrooms (Stein, Grover, & Henningsen, 1996; Stein, Lane, & Silver, 1996). Republished with permission of the National Council of Teachers of Mathematics, from Smith & Stein, 1998; permission conveyed through Copyright Clearance Center, Inc.

Examples of the task types include the following:

Lower-Level Demands (Memorization)

- Primary (K–2) Level:

$3 + 4 = ?$

- Intermediate/Middle (3–8) Level:

What is the formula for the area of a rectangle?

Lower-Level Demands (Procedures Without Connections)

- Primary (K–2) Level:

$27 + 15 = ?$

- Intermediate/Middle (3–8) Level:

$\frac{7}{8} \div 2 = ?$

Higher-Level Demands (Procedures With Connections)

- Primary (K–2) Level:

Use place value blocks to represent the following comparison question. Which is greater, 79 or 57? Show how you know.

- Intermediate/Middle (3–8) Level:

Use a number line to show $\frac{1}{4} \times \frac{1}{2} = ?$

Higher Level Demands (Doing Mathematics)

- Primary (K–2) Level:

The drive from Erin's house to school was 2 miles, and it was 4 miles from the school to the library, but only 3 miles from the library back to Erin's house. If Erin's mother drove her to school, then picked her up and took her to the library and then back home, how many miles would she travel? Be prepared to show or tell how you solved this problem.

- Intermediate/Middle (3–8) Level:

> Create a word problem for the following: 6 × 0.25.

Webb's Depth of Knowledge (DOK) model (1997) is often used to analyze the cognitive demand of assessment tasks. The DOK levels are as follows:

1. Recall and Reproduction
2. Skills and Concepts
3. Short-Term Strategic Thinking
4. Extended Thinking

The DOK levels, not unlike the Levels of Demand presented in the mathematics task analysis guide (Figure 5.1), are helpful as you consider the level of cognitive demand of the mathematical tasks you locate, repurpose, or create for your students.

The actual focus of your lesson very much dictates the level of task that you will use for your exit task. There are times when an exercise that might be considered low-level—or recall and reproduction, if you prefer using the DOK levels—is an appropriate exit task capstone to a lesson. Our hope is that all lessons engage students in doing mathematics, thus promoting regular use of problem-based, high-level or thinking-related mathematics tasks as your exit tasks.

Spangler et al. (2014) discuss the potential of the "open-middle" task. One could suggest that such tasks are a variation of an open-ended task—one in which there are many possible solutions with seemingly endless routes to a solution. In contrast, the open-middle task has one correct solution, but the task, as presented, allows multiple paths to the solution. Consider the following:

> Lucy and her family were driving to a vacation site. They would need to drive about 450 miles to reach their destination. If they drove for two days and drove close to the same amount of miles each day, how many miles could they have driven each day? Be prepared to discuss your reasoning.

Note that as long as the students arrive at a total of about 450 miles, they can provide different distances for each day, as long as each day's mileage is close to the same. The open-middle task has great

EXIT TASKS

potential as an exit task. Why? Time efficiency. Nanette Johnson, Robert Kaplinsky, and Bryan Anderson created "Open Middle" (http://www.openmiddle.com), an online repository of K–12 open-middle tasks tagged by grade, domain, CCSS-M standard, and DOK level.

Knowing that there is one, just one, solution to the exit task allows you to spend time considering the routes or paths your students used to arrive at their solution. This is not to imply that you should not use open-ended tasks, but issues related to efficiency with regard to the use of exit tasks must be considered.

The exit task is the formative assessment closer of your day. It provides demonstration or documentation of student performance on a task of particular importance for the day's lesson. Consider the connection between Show Me and the exit task. Both provide a performance-based documentation of what your students can do mathematically. While Show Me is used more frequently with individual students or small groups of students, the exit task is typically for all students, although you could differentiate tasks for particular students.

What about feedback? Should you provide feedback to your students for any of the Formative 5? Absolutely. As you use observations, interviews, and Show Me, you will provide oral feedback and written comments as appropriate, and keep records for your own planning and instructional next steps. In addition, as you regularly use hinge questions, you will collect notes on students using a variety of record-keeping tools. The information you collect will allow you to better anticipate, adjust, and provide feedback to students. As you select particular exit tasks, you will need to carefully review and decide how you will provide feedback to your students; most teachers provide comments as feedback. The exit task provides actual work samples for you to not only review, but also keep on hand to assist in planning future lessons as well as add to your mental and documented folder of the progress of each of your students. It's your almost-every-day performance assessment. Now let's get to the how and why of the exit task.

Planning for Using Exit Tasks

As noted earlier, like Show Me, the exit task provides a sampling of student performance. Exit tasks provide a record for you to monitor particular student, small group, and class performance. Coupled together, the hinge question and exit task bring mathematical closure to your lesson and provide the seeds for planning and instruction related to tomorrow's lesson and future lessons. You will plan for use of a particular exit task prior to its implementation, which would occur toward the end of the mathematics lesson of the day. Different from the hinge questions, exit tasks will require more response time for students to demonstrate their understandings. The purpose of the exit task is two-fold. First, you will provide students with an opportunity to demonstrate what they know and understand, which will help you plan and design your next steps instructionally. Second, you may use the exit task to provide explicit feedback to your students. As you create and select these tasks, you may also want to think about how you will provide feedback to your students. Consider the commentary below involving Claudia and Darshan and their use of the exit task.

> Claudia and I teach in the same school, but she teaches fifth grade and I teach kindergarten. I use an exit task with my kindergartners at the end of math time almost every day. As I plan my next day's lesson, I think about where my class should be at the end of my lesson and then 'get' a task that I think is appropriate. I get a task by going to my files or to websites I particularly like. For example, some of the sites I routinely visit include the following:
>
> - NCTM Illuminations: https://illuminations.nctm.org
> - Inside Mathematics: http://www.inside mathematics.org/performance-assessment-tasks
> - Illustrative Mathematics: https://www.illustrativemathematics.org
> - YouCubed: https://www.youcubed.org/tasks
>
> I remember picking up a task at a school district workshop using digit or number cards. I knew that I wanted to open up the task to encourage a wider range of student responses. I showed Claudia the original task and my revision:

Original Task

Alane has the following number cards: 4, 9, and 12.

- Make a set for each number.
- Which set has the most? The least?

Revised Task

Alane has the following number cards: 4, 9, and 12.

- Show each number with cubes or a drawing.

- With cubes or a drawing, make a new group that is between 9 and 12.

- Order all the numbers on a number line.

- If Alane added 2 to each group, what are the new numbers?

- Would adding two to each number change the order on the number line?

I like to use the sites noted because they can really jump-start my thinking. Our district also has links to other great sources. Oh, and I often just create my own tasks. After adapting tasks for a couple of years, I've gotten pretty good at creating my own exit tasks.

—DARSHAN

Darshan's kindergarten teaching team and my fifth-grade team got paired together at our last faculty meeting when we talked about the Formative 5. What a riot, since we represent the bookends of the school! We decided to talk about exit tasks, and I listened to what Darshan said above, but of course, I have my own take. Like Darshan, I often used sites I have found or that the school district provides to locate tasks. Like Darshan, I tend to adapt a task to fit my needs. It's funny. We both agreed that at 9 p.m. or so, or whenever we do our planning, it's much more likely that I will go to a site I trust and locate a task online and download it to jump-start my exit task development. I basically have one major question and three criteria for tasks I select:

Does this task connect directly to my plans for the day?

1. Is the mathematics appropriate?

2. Does the task engage the Standards for Mathematical Practice important to this lesson?

3. Is the level of learning/engagement of the task—low or high or DOK 1–4—appropriate?

In our fifth-grade- and kindergarten-level discussions, it was also interesting to note that both levels liked the same online sources for tasks, with each of us having other favorite sites. One difference, though. Our tasks at the fifth-grade level tend to be pretty involved—almost always high-level tasks—so I don't use the exit task every day. I use an exit task, for the most part, three days a week—Monday, Wednesday, and Friday. That gives me time to read, review, provide feedback to the students, and plan my next steps.

—CLAUDIA

I was really glad that Claudia brought up the point about particular websites she and others like—actually, the word should be trust. This has become a bit of a sticky issue in our team. One of our members regularly uses a website where she has to pay for tasks. We finally pointed out that a lot of what she was bringing to us were just fancy worksheets. The mathematics tasks seemed like fun, but didn't match the standard indicated and frankly were just exercises. We finally decided we would only gather tasks from the sites that were reputable and indicated support from experts in the field of mathematics education.

—DARSHAN

Darshan and Claudia's discussion of their use of the exit task addresses many of the everyday questions about the use of the exit task that you will confront. As you plan for your use of observations, interviews, Show Me, hinge questions, and exit tasks, one difference is that there are many online and print resources that you will be able to consider as resources for exit tasks. The questions provided in Figure 5.2 should help to guide your thinking regarding selection, creation, and use of the exit task.

Responses to the statements and questions provided in Figure 5.2 should also help guide your thinking about the use of the exit task and the resources that may be helpful to you in creating or adapting tasks for classroom use. Important considerations to keep in mind include the following:

- The exit task is the final activity assessment-wise in the lesson; to an extent, it's a whole class Show Me activity.

- You should provide time for all students to complete the exit task, since this is typically NOT a speeded activity.

- If you complete a particularly important topic during your math lesson, you may want to consider presenting the exit task then, rather than waiting until the end of your math time. This decision is mostly related to the pace of your teaching and your own comfort, and that of your students, in responding to exit tasks.

- The exit task assesses important mathematics and is often a high-level task (see the earlier discussion) that intersects important mathematics and particular Standards for Mathematical Practice (NGA Center & CCSSO, 2010).

- You may not want to use an exit task each day, since the task responses will need to be analyzed and considered for your next steps planning-wise.

- Exit task responses provide a record of student performance and can be kept for parent conferences and longer term analysis.

- Your grade-level team or school-based learning community may consider organizing and regularly updating exit tasks for use within various grade levels in the school.

Figure 5.2 • Planning for the Exit Task

1. How will you consider using an exit task?

- The exit task provides an end-of-lesson record of individual student performance. How will you analyze individual student, small group, and entire class responses?
- How will you use the analysis of exit task responses in considering particular student or class differentiation decisions?

2. Where do I get these exit tasks?

- Does your grade-level learning community or school have particular resources that you use for mathematics tasks?
  - o What are your favorite sites and resources for mathematics tasks?
- What is your comfort level with creating your own exit tasks or adapting tasks you have located online or from print resources you may have?
- Consider the following criteria when you select tasks, particularly online or previously published tasks.
  - o Is the mathematics appropriate as an exit task for this lesson? Does it match what I have taught or will teach?
  - o How will the task engage my students?
  - o Is the task *appropriately* challenging (see the discussion of levels of tasks and the DOK provided in the previous section of this chapter)?

(Continued)

EXIT TASKS

Figure 5.2 • (Continued)

○ Will I be able to use the results to guide my planning and teaching, and also use the results as a component of my ongoing record of student progress?

3. How will you plan for use of the exit task?

- As you plan for the day, what mathematics will be assessed using an exit task?
- Will the task be a lower level or DOK 1, 2 task, or a higher level or DOK 3, 4 task?
- How will you check for the mathematics content and/or mathematical practices being addressed in the exit task?
- During math time, when will your students complete the exit task?
  ○ If you complete an important component of your mathematics lesson prior to the end of mathematics time, will you use your exit task then or wait until the end of mathematics time?
- How will you use exit task results in your own planning for future lessons?

4. Given your class needs and the value of the exit task, is this a formative assessment technique that you will use every day? Several days a week?

5. How will you summarize student responses and provide feedback for your exit tasks?

- Do you have record-keeping tools that you have found to be helpful as a way to record or summarize student responses to mathematics tasks?
- How do you plan to provide comments to students as feedback on their exit task solutions and related responses?
- When will you provide feedback to your students on their exit tasks?
- How much time will you need to discuss the feedback with your students? When will you do this?
- How will you endeavor to provide a balance between supportive and constructively critical comments in the feedback you provide to your students?

6. How will you organize your classroom to implement the exit task?

- How much time will your students need to complete the exit task?
- What resources (e.g., manipulative materials, drawings, paper, online access) will be needed by students completing the exit task?
- Are there any special seating arrangements needed for use of the exit task?

Tools for Using Exit Tasks in the Classroom

As you begin to plan for and use exit tasks in your classroom, you will think about how and when to use the exit task in your lesson and how you will regularly plan for and create or adapt a task. You will also need to validate the mathematical importance of your task, ensuring a strong connection to your lesson and its intersection with the Standards for Mathematical Practice. Consider the following classroom challenges, classroom-based responses, and tools for planning for and using exit tasks.

1. **Do I use the exit task every day?**

   Classroom-Based Response: *My primary grade (K–2) teachers use an exit task every day. They review student performance each evening, and the responses guide their planning. At Grades 3–5 and the middle school level, my teachers use the exit task three days a week, typically Mondays, Wednesdays, and Fridays. At these grade levels, the sophistication of the mathematics and the time needed to review exit task responses are such that using the tasks a few days a week seems to work best.*

2. **How can I plan for using exit tasks?**

   Classroom-Based Response: *I'm a second-grade teacher and have used the Planning: Exit Tasks Tool (Figure 5.3 on the next page) for the past few months, and particularly when I began using exit tasks, I found the tool to be really helpful. Now, for the most part, I just refer to it as I plan for, determine, and implement my exit tasks.*

3. **What about feedback? When and how much?**

   Classroom-Based Response: *One of the things I found out pretty quickly is that I need to find time to quickly review the exit tasks of my students. I always provide feedback to my sixth-grade students, and I try to offer statements that support the responses of my students and offer assistance as needed. So, for example, for Caroline's exit task response for the exit task below involving volume, which I adapted from a fifth-grade-level Illustrative Mathematics task (https://www .illustrativemathematics.org/content-standards/5/MD/C/ tasks/1031), I was able to quickly see that Caroline indicated the number of grams of flour the second box could hold (240 g). Then, and I often do this, I asked for a "how do you know" response. This often pushes a lower level task that I use into the higher level range. Caroline's response was, "I found the volume of the first box, which was 30 cubic centimeters. Then I found that the volume of the second box was 180 cubic centimeters, so it was 6 times bigger." My feedback to her was very positive*

Figure 5.3 • Planning: Exit Tasks Tool

Date: October 7	**Mathematics Standard:** Write time from analog and digital clocks to the nearest 5 minutes using a.m. and p.m.	**Task Level (circle one):** Lower Level Demand (Memorization) Lower Level Demand (Procedures Without Connections)
Grade Level: 2	**Mathematical Practices:** Make sense of problems; use appropriate tools; attend to precision	Higher Level Demand (Procedures With Connections) Higher Level Demand (Doing Mathematics)

Task: Larry left the house at 4:15 p.m. His bus came 10 minutes later. When did the bus come? (Write the time and show the time using your analog clock.)

Expected Response: 4:25 p.m.; the analog clock will show the short hand on the 4 and the longer hand on the 5.

Summary of Class Responses: I wasn't overly surprised, but most students were able to determine the digital time. However, some (about 7) were challenged by having to set the analog time.

My Planning—Next Steps: We will do activities setting analog clocks tomorrow, and I will observe and use interviews and Show Me as needed to monitor student progress.

 A blank template version of this figure is available for download at
http://resources.corwin.com/Formative5

with regard to noting that the second box could hold 180 grams, but I also asked her to tell me how her "how do you know" response of 180 cubic centimeters connected with her original answer of 240 grams. I often summarize particular feedback points and use them for interviews with a student or small group of students, which is what I did with Caroline. She very quickly saw that she hadn't really completed her answer and just applied her "6 times bigger" comment incorrectly to show an expected capacity of 240 grams.

Rita had a box 2 cm high, 3 cm wide, and 5 cm long. It can hold 30 g of flour. A second box has twice the height, three times the width, and the same length as the first box. How many grams of flour can it hold? Write a "how do you know" sentence explaining your answer.

4. **What about the levels of demand of my tasks?**

> **Classroom-Based Response:** *When I first began using the exit task, I thought it was not that big of a deal. I mean, I had been using exit slips for years. But then when we began talking in grade-level groups, I came to the conclusion that my exit slips were maybe too quick and most always at a low level. Our whole school spent some time with both Webb's Dimensions of Learning (1997) and Smith and Stein's (1998) taxonomy of mathematical tasks. An activity we ended up doing, first with my fifth-grade-level team members, was to present a task to the team and then have them determine if the response demand was lower level (memorization or procedures without connections) or higher level (procedures with connections or doing mathematics). Later, we did this as a whole staff activity, which was a challenge at first, because if you hadn't taught at a particular grade level, it was hard to determine the mathematical response demand of the task. Our grade-level groups now have online files, which are used regularly, and that include for each task the mathematics content standard addressed and whether it provides for lower or higher level demand. And, while our school district does not use the DOK (Webb, 1997), I have friends who use the DOK levels similarly to the way we use the Smith and Stein taxonomy of tasks.*

As you begin to regularly use exit tasks, it will be important to keep them organized for future use. The Exit Task Organizer Tool (Figure 5.4 on the next page) can be adapted for your grade-level team or school and form the basis for online accessible files that you can use as exit tasks are located, created, adapted, and used. Ask your teacher colleagues to complete this brief form and attach it to tasks they have found, created, or used. As they use and adapt the tasks, they can add additional notes, feedback, and even advice for administering the task.

The examples that follow, one at the second-grade level and the other at the sixth-grade level, provide exit tasks and student responses and address everyday considerations for use of the exit tasks.

Grade 2—Understanding Place Value: Jenna checked her files and located some tasks to review for her lessons during the week on the following place value standard:

> 2.NBT.A.1—Understand that the three digits of a three-digit number represent amounts of hundreds, tens, and ones; e.g., 706 equals 7 hundreds, 0 tens, and 6 ones.

Figure 5.4 • Exit Task Organizer Tool

Grade Level: *3*	Dates Used: *April 14*	Today's Date: *April 26*

Mathematics Standard: *Partition shapes into parts with equal areas. Express the area of each part as a unit fraction of the whole.*

Mathematical Practices Engaged (check those that apply):

☑ 1. Make sense of problems and persevere in solving them.

☐ 2. Reason abstractly and quantitatively.

☐ 3. Construct viable arguments and critique the reasoning of others.

☐ 4. Model with mathematics.

☑ 5. Use appropriate tools strategically.

☐ 6. Attend to precision.

☐ 7. Look for and make use of structure.

☐ 8. Look for and express regularity in repeated reasoning.

Task Level (circle one):

1. Lower Level Demand (Memorization)

2. Lower Level Demand (Procedures Without Connections)

3. Higher Level Demand (Procedures With Connections)

4. Higher Level Demand (Doing Mathematics)

Exit Task: *Shade $\frac{2}{3}$ of the area of the rectangles below 2 different ways. Tell how you know that what you shaded is $\frac{2}{3}$*

Exit Task's Solution: *Drawings need to show 4 of 6 parts of the rectangular region shaded.*

Differentiation Decisions: *Will convene a small group of those students who could not determine $\frac{2}{3}$ of the rectangles for an interview. Others will begin instruction involving equivalent fractions using number line representations.*

Suggestions for Exit Task Revision: *Could use other shapes and fractions. For Grade 4, could consider equivalent fractions to $\frac{2}{3}$ using the number line.*

Comments: *Used this with both rectangular and circular regions (Eric; April 15)*

 A blank template version of this figure is available for download at
http://resources.corwin.com/Formative5

Jenna wanted to select just the right exit task for her lesson.

First, let's consider Jenna's task choices:

A.
Julio and Mark are arguing about who has the largest number. Help them out! Show your thinking and prove who has more.

Julio	Mark
3 hundreds	5 tens
2 tens	1 hundred
9 ones	6 ones

B.
Choose from the values below to create a number with a value between 300 and 600. How many combinations can you find? Use base ten blocks or draw pictures to show your work.

83 ones   56 tens   5 hundreds   9 ones

2 ones and 8 tens   27 ones

6 tens and 12 ones

32 ones and 2 hundreds   4 ones and 3 hundreds

C.
How many groups of one hundred are in the following number? How many groups of ten? Draw a picture or use base ten blocks to show how you know.

534

D.
Name the value of each of the digits in the number below.

797

Jenna recently wrote Task A after seeing something similar in her math textbook's supplemental materials. She used both Task B and Task C last year during her place value unit and hasn't used Task D since she learned about the difference between an exit ticket and an exit task. Jenna reflected for a moment about how she used to regularly use exit tickets mostly because she thought that was how she was supposed to end every math class. She knew that she actually gathered very little information from her students in those days and now loves how using exit tasks has provided her with a much better and deeper understanding of what her students know. As she locates or creates exit tasks, Jenna finds it helpful to consider the cognitive demand of each of her tasks. She usually likes to do this in collaboration with her teammates, so she asked Hannah and Ted to take a look. After some robust discussion, they decided that Tasks A, B, and C all represented higher levels of cognitive demand (procedures with connections).

Jenna wanted to see if her students could reason about the place value beyond just looking at the place of the digits; she had plenty of evidence that they could do this. With this in mind, she narrowed her choices down to Task A and Task B. While she really loved Task A, she decided it would be better as a hinge question.

She also felt that students should be able to answer Task A quickly and she could assess if students were using their understanding about place value or just using order to record the value. Jenna chose Task B because she felt that the task responses could help her in assessing her students' reasoning about place value. She also liked that Task B offered great differentiation opportunities. She was curious to see how students would put together multiple combinations. Next, she knew she would need to dedicate some real time for students to mess around with this task. She would walk around while they were completing the task and take notes while the students were working. She would note when, if, and how students used manipulatives and if particular students needed additional assistance to complete the task. She was particularly interested in a few of her students who were still struggling with the use of base ten blocks. She has seen a couple of them count the ones on a ten stick several times and this concerned her, while others were able to mentally combine place values. She was excited that this task provided so many entry points.

Jenna mentally checked her exit task list:

- ☑ Involves appropriate mathematics
- ☑ Is a high cognitive task
- ☑ Differentiates for multiple learners
- ☑ Promotes reasoning about place value

She was ready to go! She decided to give the exit task after a quick Show Me activity using digit cards. The pre-exit task Show Me was helpful as a verbal rehearsal for the exit task, and she has found that many students need it. She wanted to make sure students had plenty of time to show their thinking and understanding about place. She would use this information to plan some targeted lessons for individuals and groups. She wanted to know the following:

- Could her students combine multiple place values to create new numbers?
- How do her students represent their thinking?
- Can her students still recognize the value of the number when it is presented in different sequences (e.g., 2 ones and 8 tens)?
- How do her students build the values?

After providing the exit task, Jenna reflected on the students' work. Overall, she was pleased that most students were able to build at least two combinations. Four students struggled to reason through

6 tens and 12 ones and recognize that the value was 72, which concerned her. While most students were able to combine values using number bonds (e.g., 60 + 12 = 72), quite a few still needed base ten blocks to construct the values. Three other students flew through the exit task, and she will need to consider particular next steps for them. Her plan was to move on to work with three-digit addition and subtraction, but after reviewing the exit task results, she decided one or two more days on place value was needed. After all, place value is a critical concept for second graders.

She took a deep breath and thought about how far she had come from a few years ago when she gave exit tickets almost every day. She knew so much more about her students' mathematical conceptual understanding and thinking now. She knew that use of the exit task was making a huge difference in her planning and teaching.

Grade 6—Understand Ratio Concepts and Use Ratio Reasoning: Nevan, a Grade 6 mathematics teacher, and his students had been working on solving real-world and mathematical ratio and rate problems (6.RP.A.3). Nevan had closely observed his students' reasoning supported by the use of Show Me opportunities involving representations, which included tables of equivalent ratios, tape diagrams, double number line diagrams, or equations. Nevan had hoped to include the use of an exit task in today's lesson. Having attended a recent NCTM Annual Conference where he learned about the Open Middle website (http://www.openmiddle.com), Nevan was eager to try the Grade 6 "Finding Equivalent Ratios" (DOK 2: Skill/Concept) problem, submitted to the site by Graham Fletcher (Figure 5.5).

Figure 5.5 • Finding Equivalent Ratios

Use the digits 1-9 to create 3 equivalent ratios.
Note: Each digit can only be used once.

$$\_ : \_ = \_\,\_ : \_\,\_ = \_\,\_ : \_\,\_$$

Source: Finding Equivalent Ratios (http://www.openmiddle.com/finding-equivalent-ratios), from OpenMiddle.com, Graham Fletcher © 2015. Reprinted with permission.

Nevan reviewed the levels of demand described by the Smith and Stein mathematics task analysis guide (Figure 5.1). He noticed the potential for higher level cognitive demand of the task

- required nonalgorithmic thinking;
- required students to explore and understand the nature of the concept of equivalent ratios;

- demanded self-monitoring or self-regulation of one's own cognitive processes; and

- required students to examine task constraints that may limit possible solutions and strategies (i.e., using digits 1 through 9 and each digit only once).

With about seven or eight minutes left in the class period, Nevan introduced the problem, giving each student a large index card to record solutions and show his or her work. Of course, Nevan had completed the problem himself while planning the lesson, but he was pleased to see that more than 75 percent of his students had created representations involving the use of ratio tables (which he himself had not even considered) as they worked within the constraints of using each of the nine numbers only once to create three equivalent ratios. As Nevan collected the task, two students indicated that they had not finished. No problem, they would be allowed to take the task home and submit via email or first thing in the morning. Nevan reflected on the use of this particular exit task, thinking about how he might make it better next time. One consideration was to perhaps add a Show Me request involving the explicit student use of a ratio table in addition to any other approach or method used to solve the exit task. Either way, Nevan was pleased with the persistence of his students as he recalled that in the beginning of the year, several had often given up on problems requiring any type of considerable cognitive effort.

Technology Tools and Tips for Exit Tasks

There are several websites mentioned throughout this chapter with mathematical tasks that hold good potential for use as exit tasks. There are also some promising tools that provide teachers with the opportunity to pose, capture, and analyze student responses to exit tasks. Many of those mentioned in the Show Me (Chapter 3) and hinge question (Chapter 4) chapters have potential use with exit tasks too (e.g., CueThink, Google Forms, Formative, Padlet). Another popular tool is Socrative (www.socrative.com), which, among other features, allows teachers to choose or develop exit tasks, view live student responses, receive questions from students, discuss results, or ask more follow-up questions.

The power in using exit tasks with or without digital technology is in how the information collected about student performance is used. A true benefit of using digital tools with the Formative 5 techniques is having the ability to capture, share, compare, and review responses over time. The convenience of being able to seamlessly analyze and rewind, using the technology as a means to efficiently provide students with meaningful feedback, is so important to your planning and teaching. Opportunities afforded only through using technology often provide your class with the ability to see all student responses, giving your students a chance to provide each other with feedback, learn from misconceptions and errors, and share understandings with each other.

Using Exit Tasks in YOUR Classroom

As with each of the Formative 5 techniques, considerations for use of the exit task will be an important element of your lesson planning. The exit task caps major concepts or skills presented within your lesson, and, as noted previously, the exit task and hinge question provide mathematical closure to your lesson. As with observations, interviews, Show Me, and the hinge question, student responses to the exit task help to identify the instructional needs of your students. As you plan for the next day's lesson, include considerations related to grouping and differentiation. Related to the more individualized or small group Show Me technique, the exit task provides a sampling of actual student performance. The more experience you have with the use of the exit task, the less time it will take you to create, adapt, or locate viable exit tasks, present and review them, and provide feedback to your students. However, regular use of the exit task includes the following time-demanding elements:

- Locating or creating a task related to your mathematics lesson; considering the mathematics content, the Standards for Mathematical Practice engaged, the level of demand of the task, and the time needed for your students to complete the task

- Presenting the exit task to your students

- Reviewing and analyzing student responses to the exit task

- Providing feedback to your students based on their response to the exit task

- Adapting your planning and teaching based on exit task responses

EXIT TASKS

Rich: I use the exit task a lot. Not every day, but most days. The fifth- and sixth-grade teaching teams at our intermediate school often plan our exit tasks together. While we plan, we think about the important "hot spots" of our lessons, making sure that both our hinge question and exit task address these major elements of these lessons. Whenever I do my final "dry run" for my lesson, I think about the extent to which my students should be ready for the exit task as well as consider possible student responses. My hope, and that of our teaching teams, is that our exit tasks will engage our students in, for the most part, higher level tasks that regularly promote reasoning and problem solving. We also usually enter our exit tasks online and make comments about their use, if appropriate (see Figure 5.4). This helps build up the cache of tasks that we can use, along with other resources and online tasks that we can repurpose for our classrooms. To some extent, we've always used tasks. Now we know what to consider when selecting or creating tasks and how to use the exit task to advise our planning and teaching.

The tools presented in the previous section of this chapter and the teacher comments and examples provided should be helpful to you as you consider your own planning for and use of the exit task. The exit task is your end-of-lesson document of progress and provides mathematical closure for a lesson or perhaps a multiday topic. It provides a record for future use, whether updating or comparing progress from time to time, and a work sample you can use to consider grade-level differentiation efforts or share at parent conferences. Perhaps more importantly, it adds to all you know, through your everyday use of observing, interviewing, Show Me, and hinge questions, about your students' mathematical knowledge and background.

Summing Up

The exit task serves as an end-of-lesson barometer of the mathematical understandings of your students. Depending on the focus of the lesson, the exit task may assess a full range of mathematical expectations. Such tasks will more frequently address problem solving and reasoning. Reviewing student responses to your exit task should provide you with direction for your planning and instructional next steps. Monitoring the success of your exit tasks will also provide you with a regularly updated and growing collection of important tasks for future years. And, as with the other elements of the Formative 5, the continuing use of the exit task is enhanced when school or grade-level learning communities work together in their creation, use, and revision. This, the final technique of the Formative 5, completes the palette of classroom-based formative assessment techniques you will use to both monitor student progress and guide your planning and teaching every day.

Professional Learning Discussion Questions

Read and discuss the following questions with your grade-level teaching team or with teams across multiple grade levels. Take notes here or use the tools in the Book Study Guide to record your thoughts.

How frequently would you use exit tasks?

How will you provide feedback to your students with regard to their exit task performance?

How will you consider the levels of cognitive demand as you select, adapt, or create tasks?

When might you use the exit task prior to the end of a lesson that you have taught or are teaching?

How might you consider exit tasks as ongoing preassessments for summative tests you might use, like unit tests?

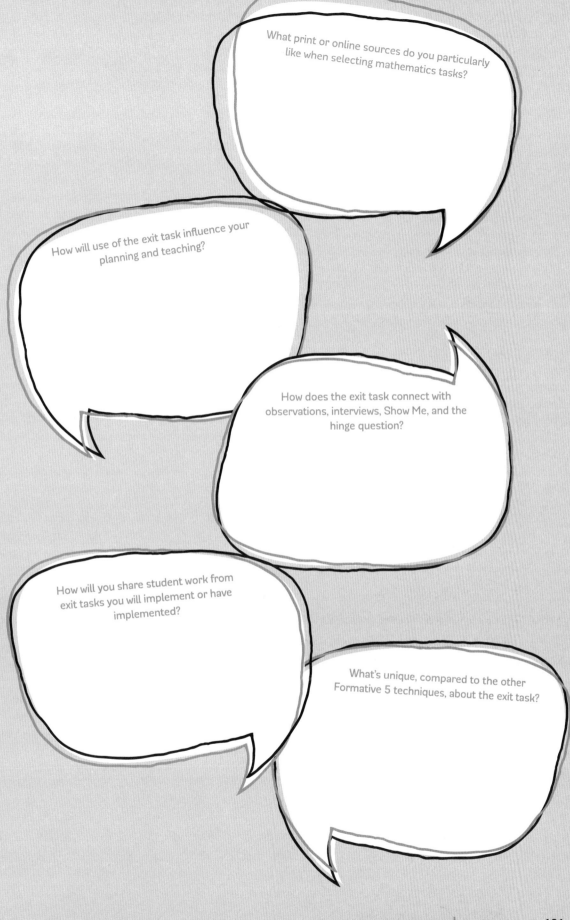

PART III

NEXT STEPS

CHAPTER 6

IT'S YOUR TURN!

Creating and defining the Formative 5, and having teachers and mathematics coaches/specialists and leaders actually use and critique the techniques, has been a multiyear effort. The previous five chapters set the stage for the intent of our efforts. Now, it's your turn. This book has discussed issues and opportunities related to formative assessment while justifying the need for and defining the techniques we call the Formative 5. The chapters specific to the observation, interview, Show Me, hinge question, and exit task techniques included sections that present questions for you to consider as you begin to plan for and use the techniques, tools for using the techniques in your classroom, and tips and tools for using technology. In a direct, in-the-classroom kind of way, we present the comments of scores of K–8 classroom teachers and mathematics coaches/specialists and leaders as they addressed the challenges for using a particular Formative 5 technique in their own classroom-based settings. Now it's your turn! Provided below is a concise and abbreviated synopsis of each of the book's chapters followed by frequently asked questions related to both statements within the chapter and those that the chapter may prompt. Consider these carefully, as the questions and the responses are meant to address any lingering concerns you may have. Finally, the chapter will conclude with specific thoughts for both implementing the Formative 5 and integrating this palette of techniques.

Why Formative Assessment? Issues and Opportunities

This section frames the book. It acknowledges the fact that you assess student progress all day long every day, emphasizing the potential of particular formative assessment techniques to inform your planning and teaching. The chapter also presents a brief orientation to the Formative 5—observations, interviews, Show Me, hinge questions, and exit tasks.

Frequently Asked Questions

Q: Why is assessment literacy important?

Response: Assessment literacy includes being able to create, select, and effectively use classroom assessments as well as being able to effectively interpret and use results from external summative assessments. In other words, it encompasses essentially ALL of your assessment responsibilities related to using assessments of any type. But it is also related to your expectations and planning around the assessments you identify, select, or create in order to monitor student growth and diagnose specific student needs. That's a lot to think about, isn't it? But it sure is important—all of it.

Q: Formative Assessment, Summative Assessment—what's the difference?

Response: Formative assessments are an integral component of every lesson and help to both monitor student progress and guide your planning and teaching. Summative assessments measure what students have learned at the end of a set of learning experiences. Such assessments include state and local school district assessments. See full definitions of both formative and summative assessment in this chapter.

Q: I didn't see this discussed—what about the Formative 5 and grading?

Response: As noted throughout this book, the Formative 5 are intended to inform your practice by guiding your planning and teaching every day and by providing a constantly updated profile of individual student and class progress in learning mathematics. Should you grade responses to any of the Formative 5 techniques? Our quick response is no, that's not the intent. Grades are the algebraic symbols of assessment, although typically upper case! They symbolically represent what you are constantly updating every minute of every classroom day—student progress. Consider the following: Would you individually grade what you observe, the interview responses of a student, or feedback to a Show Me response, hinge point question, or exit task? We think not. Our position about grading student responses to any of the Formative 5 has been framed by our concern that grading when students are initially learning a particular concept or topic is not informed grading. At this point, learning is developing and emerging as students are observed or interviewed, respond to a Show Me request, answer a hinge question, and even work through an exit task. Evaluating students as they are just learning about, exploring, and engaging with new concepts does not give a complete picture of their understanding and may contribute to student anxiety or even fear or a reluctance to perform. Additionally, grading a formative response to any of the techniques presented sends a message to students that they are expected to immediately "get" particular concepts/skills/understandings.

We do know that some teachers with whom we have worked have found a workable way to grade exit tasks. Some have even graded Show Me responses. Interestingly, both of these techniques typically provide a performance-based written response. The decision to grade student responses to an exit task or any other formative assessment is yours, but the determination, framing, and use of the Formative 5 are more about embedding assessment with planning and teaching to seamlessly address student progress and, for reasons noted, were never considered as formal grading opportunities.

Chapter 1: Observations

This chapter introduces the use of the observation as a formative assessment technique. The observations you make throughout your day inform your teaching minute by minute. Think about it. What you observe may cause you to shift a lesson's focus, alter the pace of the lesson, engage particular resources, and more. How you anticipate and use observations provides you with that initial link to how formative assessment can and will influence your planning and teaching.

Frequently Asked Questions

Q: How can what I observe be considered formative assessment?

Response: Don't underestimate the importance of what you observe. In that moment that you observe a student or students engaged in a mathematics activity, you are making a decision about what they are learning and monitoring their progress. That's assessment, and the informal nature by which you continually update your view of a student's progress using observations deepens YOUR understanding of a student's progress.

Q: I observe all the time. How do I actually plan for it, provide records of the observations, and provide feedback to my students?

Response: Well, in a word, anticipate! As you plan tomorrow's mathematics lesson, consider the focus of the mathematics content as well as the extent to which particular Standards for Mathematical Practice (e.g., problem solving, reasoning, model with mathematics) will be engaged in the lesson. Then anticipate what your students might be doing as they are involved in doing the mathematics in your lesson. That's what you will observe. Consider one or more of the tools provided in this chapter to assist you in developing a record of your observations. Also think about how you might provide feedback to your students based on what you observe. You may decide to interview one or more of your students—that's feedback. Maybe you will use Show Me, which could also involve feedback. Note how the Formative 5—in this case, observations, interviews, and Show Me—are connected to each other.

Q: When does what I observe reach the level of considering the use of an interview?

Response: As you observe your students doing mathematics, they will say or do things that will get your attention—what an understatement! Those are situations that make you wonder about what your students did and why they are obvious choices for an interview. But you should also anticipate who you may want to interview just to check in with them and provide some feedback. Once again, note the intersection between two components or colors of the Formative 5 palette, in this case, observations and interviews.

Chapter 2: Interviews

The Interviews chapter presents and discusses how and why the interview extends what you have observed. Your interview questions provide you with an everyday opportunity to deepen your understanding of what your students know. The interview responses from your students will influence the decisions you may make about how to differentiate instruction for individual students and your classroom needs as a whole. Anticipating when you may interview students within a lesson will identify lesson topics, concepts, or procedures where use of the interview technique is particularly valuable. It is important to note that the interview should not be a technique used primarily to assess deficiencies. We have found that the interview is often used to explore unique, creative, and advanced understandings and solutions to problems as well as assess student mathematical dispositions.

Frequently Asked Questions

Q: How will I have time to actually do interviews?

Response: The key to this response is related to your planning of a lesson. Anticipate potential elements of your lesson that may be new for your students, may challenge them, or may be uniquely troublesome for them based on your experience. What might you observe that would cause you to interview students? Then think about your students. Who might you want to interview? Why? These anticipatory questions help you in considering the amount of time that you may need to interview individual or small groups of students, remembering that each interview would last five minutes or less.

Q: How formal are my interviews?

Response: Your interviews should not be very formal. We all know how aware students are when they sense something is different or formal. The interview is a directed conversation. Many interviews are simply, "Tell me what you are doing and why you are doing it that way." Clinical interviews take longer and are far more involved than the lesson-centered interview technique presented as a component of the Formative 5.

Q: What should I record?

Response: You will want to keep a record of interview comments. Such comments should include actual work samples and/or audio accounts of a student's thinking. The Individual Student: Interview Prompt (Figure 2.6) and Classroom: Interview Record (Figure 2.5) are particularly helpful record-keeping tools. Some teachers also video record their interviews or use digital tools that capture both written work and the audio of student and teacher conversations. Tracking the interview comments of a student, over time, always provides an interesting account of student thinking.

Chapter 3: Show Me

Like the interview, the Show Me technique extends an observation. While you have always observed your students as they engage in mathematics learning activities and may have read about clinical interviews or planned and conducted interviews with your students, it's not likely that you have read about or used the Show Me technique. As we determined the techniques of the Formative 5, the Show Me technique evolved from our work with both observations and interviews. It became very natural for teachers to ask students to show what they were doing and, as appropriate, offer an explanation of the solution strategies used. Show Me represents a student performance often, but certainly not always, demonstrating the use of particular tools—manipulatives, drawings, or online. As with all of the Formative 5, your planning should suggest when you might actually use Show Me and how you might use this record of student performance.

Frequently Asked Questions

Q: When do I use Show Me?

Response: When you plan, you will think about and anticipate when you might use Show Me. Are there components of your proposed lesson that have seemingly always been problematic for students? Such points may be targets for Show Me. But you could also use Show Me to just spontaneously check in with students based on what you have observed, which is what makes Show Me such a valuable in-the-moment assessment tool. And of course, Show Me does provide a record of student performance that you may analyze and compare with other records of student performance.

Q: Could I have all of my students do Show Me in a lesson, or is it just for individual students or small groups of students?

Response: You can use Show Me as you monitor student progress with individual and small groups of students, and also your entire class. For instance, there may be a key concept or procedure in your lesson that you would like all of your students to demonstrate (e.g., use of double number lines to compare fractions and decimals side by side). You could have students use materials, drawings, or online tools to show their response. You will then need to invest a few minutes in checking Show Me responses. Alternatively, the Small Group: Show Me Record (Figure 3.2) could easily be adapted for the class and pictures used for actual student responses that you could check at the end of the day, if needed. The only real challenge of a whole class Show Me is circulation around the class to get a sense of the class's performance. Some teachers with whom we have worked have students use their whiteboards, holding up their responses for a quick every-pupil-response view.

Q: Are there times when what I observe may necessitate an interview and Show Me? Would I do all three?

Response: As you plan each day's mathematics lesson, you will anticipate your use of each of the Formative 5 techniques. This all starts with what you expect to observe your students doing in mathematics class that day. As you consider what you will observe, also consider what aspects of the mathematics engagement may warrant an interview. Would there also be places within the lesson where you may want to just stop whatever you are presenting and ask students to show what they are doing, and perhaps discuss why? As noted in the respective chapters, what you observe may warrant an interview. Show Me is more spontaneous but also connected to both the observation and interview. We sometimes think of Show Me as an abbreviated performance-based interview. Together, the observation, interview, and Show Me monitor the progress of your students and your lesson.

Chapter 4: Hinge Questions

As you observe, interview, or have students complete a Show Me request, you are monitoring your teaching and gathering student responses while your lesson is in progress. The hinge question seeks to assess what your students know about today's lesson. It typically occurs toward the end of a lesson or at the conclusion of particular hinge points (e.g., when shifting from one content topic to another) within the lesson. Hinge questions are diagnostic in that the responses identify the understandings and related instructional needs of your students and serve to inform and guide your next steps in both planning and teaching. Hinge questions are posed using a multiple-choice format with response choices or as a short-response question. Responses to the hinge question and analysis and interpretation of the responses should all occur in about two minutes or less.

Frequently Asked Questions

Q: How is the hinge question diagnostic?

Response: The hinge question is not a discussion question. It's diagnostic in that you are asking students about a major element of the day's lesson and seeking responses that will determine what your students know or understand. Some think of the hinge question as a whole class interview. The responses, in a sense, assess your lesson and provide direct student feedback to you as to your next steps planning-wise and instructionally.

Q: What's the difference between a hinge question and a hinge point question?

Response: There is no real difference between hinge and hinge point questions. The difference is related to their use. If your lesson is focused mostly around a single content topic, you'll ask the hinge question toward the end of your mathematics teaching time. If your lesson involves multiple mathematics topics within the same lesson, you will ask hinge point questions as you move from one mathematics topic to the next within the lesson.

Q: How much time should I allot for a hinge question?

Response: We like to think that you have a little less than a two-minute window to ask the hinge question, for your students to respond, and for you to analyze and interpret responses. Use of the multiple-choice format hinge question easily fits within this time frame.

Q: What if I want to revise my hinge question?

Response: When you plan a lesson, the finished project is always "under construction." In anticipating and even providing a hinge question or hinge point question for your lesson, it is always your responsibility to adapt when needed. This could include changing the language and focus of your hinge or hinge point questions. So, be prepared to revise hinge questions as needed.

Chapter 5: Exit Tasks

The exit task provides mathematical closure to your lesson. More challenging and engaging than the oft-used exit slip or exit ticket, the exit task will most likely address problem solving, reasoning, and other Standards for Mathematical Practice. You will need to consider how you will access, create, and/or modify exit tasks for your use. Online sites and previously published tasks may be adapted to address your needs. Since the exit task represents a written account of student performance, time will be needed to review student responses and provide feedback to your students. Collecting student exit tasks over time provides you with a trajectory of a student's mathematical accomplishments throughout the year.

Frequently Asked Questions

Q: My school expects me to address the closure of my lesson each day. Could the exit task be considered a closure activity?

Response: The exit task certainly can be considered as an integral component of a lesson's closure, which would most likely also include a summation of the lesson and a foreshadowing of tomorrow's lesson. Remember that the use of the exit task builds on what you have done throughout the lesson assessment-wise. You have observed, interviewed, used Show Me, and already asked a hinge question, so the exit task is integral to the other closure-related elements of any lesson.

Q: I wonder about finding good exit tasks for my grade level. Are there resources I should consider?

Response: First, don't think you have to create all the exit tasks you will use. There are many active websites and technological tools mentioned in Chapter 5 that you can access to help in finding and adapting tasks. Many learning communities set up grade-level resource files just for sharing their exit tasks.

Q: Given the amount of time needed to review student responses to exit tasks, should I use them every day, like the other Formative 5 techniques?

Response: That really depends on the task you use. If the task is particularly challenging for your students and their responses take a lot of time to review and provide feedback, then you may want to consider using exit tasks every other day. This truly depends on the time needed to locate, prepare, present, and review the tasks you use.

What's Next?

Well, now it's your turn. The hope and plan is for you to have read this book and discussed the Formative 5 techniques to the point where you are now ready to use them every day in your classroom. Will this be easy? Of course not. But you can do this! Will you start out using each technique every day? While that is the goal, any new initiative takes time for full and consistent implementation. We have had schools and school districts use the Formative 5. The sampling of teacher and teacher leader comments provided below by participants in these pilot implementations may be helpful to you as you consider your own challenges related to regular use of the Formative 5.

On getting started with the Formative 5

- I feel that my staff has "turned the corner" for the most part in using the Formative 5. I will be continuing the implementation next year.

- The teachers in our building are beginning to understand the shift to using the Formative 5 and making it meaningful. More time and I think the impact will be more visible.

- We really need another full year of using the Formative 5 before we will be able to make a real difference.

On using particular Formative 5 techniques

- It will take our teachers a while to become proficient with the hinge question.

- We are still working on developing and finding better exit tasks.

- With the interviews and Show Me, our students are more comfortable with explaining their thinking on assessments.

General comments about use of the Formative 5

- I don't know how people can teach without the Formative 5.

- I think my teachers have become more mindful of assessing students on a daily basis to help determine their next steps in instruction.

- My teachers feel better and more confident creating and using formative assessments.

- Our quarterly assessment scores (summative assessments) increased in the classrooms where teachers regularly used the Formative 5.

The anecdotal comments above should be helpful as reminders of both the challenges and what might be able to happen as you begin to explore your own use of the Formative 5. Consider this palette of formative assessment techniques and create your own assessment artistry each and every day. Also note that the appendix of this book provides a book study guide for your teaching team or professional learning community to consider. Additionally, an e-course for all aspects of the Formative 5 is being developed. One more time—you can do this!

APPENDIX

BOOK STUDY GUIDE

Our intent is for this book study guide to be used in collaborative learning communities within and/or across grade-level/course teams or by other interested and like-minded teachers and teacher leaders. The actual group composition for the professional learning is not important; rather, the learning community's collective goal of learning about and beginning to use the Formative 5 techniques is the key to successful integration of these assessment techniques into your daily teaching practice. In our experience with classroom teachers and mathematics leaders, we have learned that collaboration will improve the process, increase accountability for all participants, and thus provide support as you develop your own understanding of each of the Formative 5 techniques.

Before beginning this collaborative work, it is critical to establish mutually agreed-upon participation norms. This professional learning experience will invite you and other teachers to communicate ideas, try the Formative 5 assessment techniques, and share your students' work, which can be very revealing and personal for teachers. Norms provide a safe and respectful space for a learning community to take risks and share ideas, concerns, possible missteps, and successes. Norms work best if the group develops them because the members establish ownership and are more likely to adhere to such norms. As you develop these norms, consider how the learning community will want to address the following topics:

- **Time.** This may include establishing the meeting times, dealing with absences and tardiness, and developing a long-range plan for the group (e.g., *We will begin and end our book study meetings on time and maintain full focus throughout*).

- **Participation.** This may include who participates in the learning community and the ways in which they participate, particularly as this connects to sharing and listening. For example, some learning communities enforce a norm that meetings begin with a rule that *each participant must share or give an update, ensuring that all members of the learning community contribute*. Participants may also need to determine if new members may be invited to the learning community once the book study group has been established.

- **Confidentiality.** We have designed this professional development guide to encourage you to plan for and implement the Formative 5 in your own classroom as a collaborative learning community. We understand that trying new things can feel uncertain. Sometimes such implementations go well, yet other times you may feel frustrated or even disappointed in what you are learning about your students' mathematical understanding. Planning for and engaging in formative assessment can sometimes reveal critical student misconceptions that can be distracting, even overwhelming, to teachers. In other situations, you may learn that your students possess incredible mathematical strengths. We recognize that this process can be deeply personal; therefore, we recommend that confidentiality norms around student work and teacher reflection be established (e.g., *Unless stated, what is shared/discussed in our meetings remains confidential*). We feel that this norm is critical to your work.

- **Goals.** Developing one or two simple, long-range goals or outcomes that are connected to the book study will help your learning community adhere to the timeline and remain focused. You may also want to develop a norm that requires the learning community to *establish a goal for the next book study meeting to ensure that your work is progressing.*

- **Record and Resource Keeping.** We have found this to be an integral part of our work with collaborative learning communities. As you engage in planning for and using the Formative 5 assessment techniques, both during and after this book study, you will want to decide where (and how) to "house" all of the formative assessment resources and artifacts developed by your learning community. We recommend that you create a plan for storing and sharing tools, notes, and samples of student work from the Formative 5 techniques (observations, interview questions, Show Me responses, hinge questions, and exit tasks). Many of our collaborative learning communities find it easiest to store this information in a digital/online location that can be accessed only by those members of the learning community.

- **Sharing.** During and after this book study, you and your collaborative group are going to work hard to develop and implement the Formative 5 techniques. We advise that you decide how you will share this work with colleagues.

In our work with teachers and mathematics leaders, we have learned that in order to understand and begin to integrate the Formative 5 techniques into your daily teaching practice, it is best to tackle them one at a time before incorporating the next technique. For the purposes of this book study guide, we will lead you through a process of reflection, discussion, and first attempts at implementation.

Let's take a look at a sample book study you can use to read and discuss essential questions related to the Formative 5. Note that the questions provided for the book study discussion are the Professional Learning Discussion Questions provided at the end of each chapter of the book. Of course, we encourage you to alter this plan, including altering the questions, to meet your individual and collective learning community needs, and whether your discussion will happen live and in person, live online, or even online asynchronously.

THE FORMATIVE 5

Companion
Website

BOOK STUDY GUIDE

Available for download at
http://resources.corwin.com/Formative5

Formative 5 Book Study Timeline

Week	Read Chapter(s)	Date for Discussion
1	Why Formative Assessment?	
2	Chapter 1: Observations Chapter 2: Interviews	
3	Chapter 3: Show Me	
4	Chapter 4: Hinge Questions	
5	Chapter 5: Exit Tasks	

WHY FORMATIVE ASSESSMENT?
ISSUES AND OPPORTUNITIES

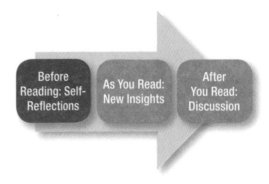
Before Reading: Self-Reflections

As You Read: New Insights

After You Read: Discussion

Before Reading: Self-Reflections.
As you prepare to read Why
Formative Assessment? Issues and
Opportunities, consider jotting
down some of your own thoughts
and ideas about assessment.

Prereading Questions	My Thoughts and Questions
1. How does (or perhaps should) the use of formative assessment influence your instructional planning?	
2. How much time do you spend each day as you assess student progress in mathematics?	
3. How much time do you spend each month *and* during the entire school year assessing your students? Make sure to include the summative assessments you administer as well as the formative assessments you may provide.	
4. In your own words, describe the differences between formative and summative assessments.	
5. What formative assessment techniques are you currently using?	
6. What concerns you the most about your use of formative assessment every day?	
7. What concerns you the most about the imbalance, particularly as emphasized in reporting to parents and in the media, between formative and summative assessment?	
8. How do you provide feedback to your students with regard to assessments that you use? Share this response with your building-based colleagues.	
9. Is there a difference between how feedback is provided that is based on the developmental level of students? Does the mathematics content being assessed impact how you provide feedback?	

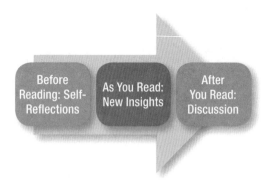

As You Read: New Insights.
When working with a collaborative team, it is often very helpful to be prepared with notes about the reading. Use the following chart to record your notes.

Thoughts on Why Formative Assessment? Issues and Opportunities					
Reading Notes	Page	I wonder...	This connects to...	I'd like to try...	I am worried about...

Before Reading: Self-Reflections

As You Read: New Insights

After You Read: Discussion

After You Read: Discussion. The chapter Why Formative Assessment? Issues and Opportunities introduces formative assessment beginning with a discussion of assessment literacy. After reading this section, begin your group session by sharing some of your thoughts about the reading. You may begin by revisiting the discussion questions introduced in the Before Reading section. You may use the following graphic organizer to record your ideas from the group discussion regarding sharing, identifying particular Aha! moments from the group, and then determining the next steps (Let's Try!) for individuals or the group. As the group shares, each participant can record interesting thoughts, summaries, or new questions developed from the reading. The Aha! section is a place to record new insights, and Let's Try! is the actionable item that the group will want to try after reading and discussing the chapter.

Sharing	Aha!	Let's Try!

Before Reading: Self-Reflections. As you prepare to read Chapter 1: Observations, take a minute to jot down some of your own thoughts and ideas about the questions below. Then revisit them as you share and discuss.

Prereading Questions	My Thoughts and Questions
1. How often do you actually use observation? Would you consider your use of observation as formative assessment?	
2. How might you use observation every day to monitor your students as you teach and as they learn mathematics?	
3. In thinking about what you expect to observe, also think about how you would know "it" (what you expect) when you saw it. What will you do if you don't see "it," or students don't do what you expect?	
4. When would you actually make notes about what you have observed in your mathematics classroom?	
5. Which of the observation tools in this chapter might you use or adapt and use in your own classroom? What observation tools have you created or used?	

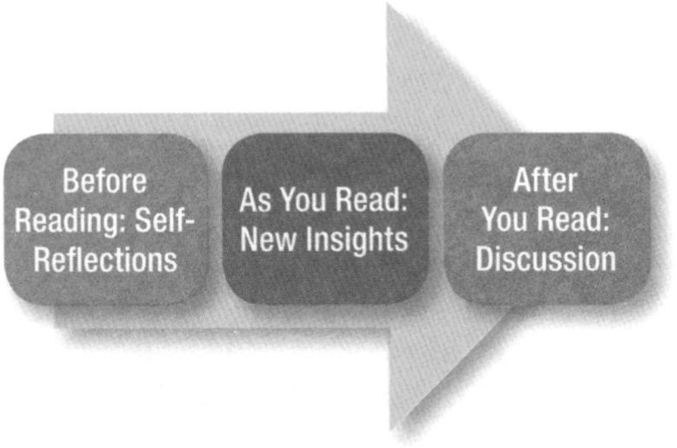

Before Reading: Self-Reflections

As You Read: New Insights

After You Read: Discussion

As You Read: New Insights.
Use the following chart to record your notes about Chapter 1: Observations.

Thoughts on Chapter 1: Observations					
Reading Notes	Page	I wonder ...	This connects to ...	I'd like to try ...	I am worried about ...

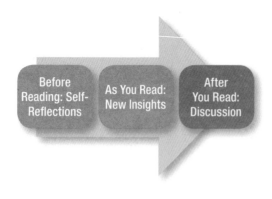

Before Reading: Self-Reflections

As You Read: New Insights

After You Read: Discussion

After You Read: Discussion. Now that you have read Chapter 1: Observations and considered the Professional Learning Discussion Questions, you may revisit them as a guide to organizing your discussion. We suggest that you record relevant ideas from the group discussion in the graphic organizer below. Make sure to identify particular Aha! moments, and then some actionable items for individual participants or groups to actually try (Let's Try)!

Sharing	Aha!	Let's Try!

CHAPTER 2: INTERVIEWS

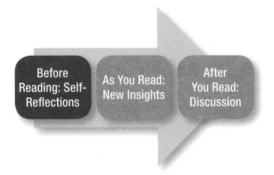

Before Reading: Self-Reflections.
As you prepare to read Chapter 2: Interviews, make a note of some of your own thoughts and ideas about conducting interviews.

Prereading Questions	My Thoughts and Questions
1. Have you used interviews in your classroom? If so, how has their use impacted your planning and teaching?	
2. What challenges do you envision as you think about daily use of the interview technique?	
3. Which of the interview tools provided in this chapter would you use or adapt and use in your classroom?	
4. How would you describe the link between your use of observation of mathematics teaching and the use of interviews in your classroom?	
5. Think about one particular student you have and a recent or forthcoming lesson. How would that student would respond to the following interview questions? *How did you do that?* *Tell me why you did "that" (e.g., solved that problem) that way.*	

As You Read: New Insights. Use the following chart to record your notes about Chapter 2: Interviews.

Thoughts on Chapter 2: Interviews					
Reading Notes	Page	I wonder...	This connects to...	I'd like to try...	I am worried about...

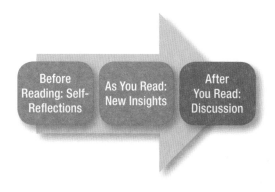

After You Read: Discussion. Chapter 2 introduces interviewing as a formative assessment technique. After reading the chapter, begin your group session by sharing some of your thoughts about the reading. As with the previous chapters, you may begin by revisiting the discussion questions introduced in the Before Reading section. Use the graphic organizer below to record your ideas from the group discussion, identify particular Aha! moments from the group, and then determine the next steps (Let's Try!) for individuals or the group. As the group shares, participants can record interesting thoughts, summaries, or new questions developed from the reading. The Aha! section is a place to record new insights and the Let's Try! is the actionable item that the group will want to try after reading and discussing the chapter.

Sharing	Aha!	Let's Try!

CHAPTER 3: SHOW ME

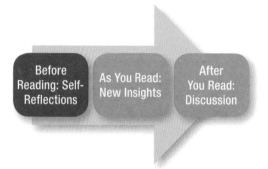

Before Reading: Self-Reflections.
As you prepare to read Chapter 3: Show Me, jot down some of your own thoughts and ideas about the questions below. Then make sure to revisit them as you share and discuss.

Prereading Questions	My Thoughts and Questions
1. How do you envision using a Show Me assessment in your classroom?	
2. What challenges do you envision as you consider daily use of the Show Me technique?	
3. Which of the Show Me examples provided in this chapter would you use or adapt for use in your classroom?	
4. Are there particular lessons that you think would more likely engage many more Show Me opportunities than other lessons? Which? Why do you think so?	
5. How would you describe the connection between observing, interviewing, and use of Show Me? How might this connection impact both your planning and teaching?	
6. In your grade-level team, consider the major mathematics topics at your particular grade level. Spend time creating at least one Show Me prompt for each of these topics, making sure to find the time to share and discuss the prompts.	

As You Read: New Insights. Use the chart below to record your notes about your reading of Chapter 3: Show Me.

Thoughts on Chapter 3: Show Me					
Reading Notes	Page	I wonder…	This connects to…	I'd like to try…	I am worried about…

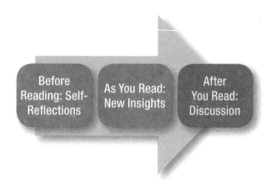

Before Reading: Self-Reflections

As You Read: New Insights

After You Read: Discussion

After You Read: Discussion. Chapter 3 introduces the Show Me formative assessment technique as a way to quickly assess student performance. After reading the chapter, begin your group session by sharing some of your thoughts about the reading. As with previous chapter discussions, begin by revisiting the discussion questions introduced in the Before Reading section. Use the graphic organizer below to record your ideas from the group discussion, identify particular Aha! moments from the group, and then determine the next steps (Let's Try!) for individuals or the group. As the group shares, each participant can record interesting thoughts, summaries, or new questions developed from the reading. As noted previously, the Aha! section is a place to record new insights, and the Let's Try! is the actionable item that the group will want to try after reading and discussing the chapter.

Sharing	Aha!	Let's Try!

CHAPTER 4: HINGE QUESTIONS

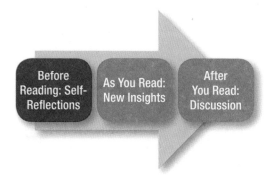

Before Reading: Self-Reflections.
As you prepare to read Chapter 4: Hinge Questions, jot down some of your own thoughts and ideas about the questions below. Revisit them as you share and discuss the chapter.

Prereading Questions	My Thoughts and Questions
1. How will you consider creating hinge questions as you plan your mathematics lessons?	
2. What every-student-response techniques or materials might your students use as they respond to hinge questions?	
3. Are there particular content topics that may be more appropriate for the multiple-choice format of the hinge question than others?	
4. How can you use observations, interviews, and the Show Me technique to assist in your use of the hinge question?	
5. How might your learning community plan for and develop hinge questions?	
6. How might your learning community share, discuss, and reflect on student responses to hinge questions? How might it adapt them for future use?	
7. The hinge question is considered to be diagnostic, as discussed in the chapter. How does the hinge question differ from other questions you may ask of your students?	
8. How might you plan for a range of hinge questions that might be used across grade-level teams?	

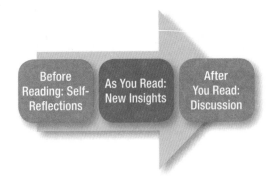

As You Read: New Insights. Use the chart below to record your notes from the chapter.

Reading Notes	Page	I wonder...	This connects to...	I'd like to try...	I am worried about...

Before Reading: Self-Reflections

As You Read: New Insights

After You Read: Discussion

After You Read: Discussion. Chapter 4 introduces the hinge question formative assessment technique as a critical question that helps you both assess student progress within a lesson and make instructional decisions. After reading this chapter, begin your group session by sharing some of your thoughts about the reading. You may begin by revisiting the discussion questions introduced in the Before Reading section. As with previous chapters, use the following graphic organizer to record your ideas from the group discussion, identify particular Aha! moments from the group, and determine the next steps (Let's Try!) for individuals or the group. As the group shares, each participant can record interesting thoughts, summaries, or new questions developed from the reading. The Aha! section is a place to record new insights, and the Let's Try! is the actionable item that the group will want to try after reading and discussing the chapter.

Sharing	Aha!	Let's Try!

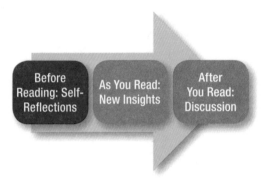

Before Reading: Self-Reflections.

As you prepare to read Chapter 5: Exit Tasks, jot down some of your own thoughts and ideas about the questions below. Revisit them as you share and discuss.

Prereading Questions	My Thoughts and Questions
1. How frequently would you use exit tasks?	
2. How will you provide feedback to your students with regard to their exit task performance?	
3. How will you consider the levels of cognitive demand as you select, adapt, or create tasks?	
4. When might you use the exit task prior to the end of a lesson that you have taught or are teaching?	
5. How might you consider exit tasks as ongoing preassessments for summative tests you might use, like unit tests?	
6. What print or online sources do you particularly like when selecting mathematics tasks?	
7. How will use of the exit task influence your planning and teaching?	
8. How does the exit task connect with observations, interviews, Show Me, and the hinge question?	
9. How will you share student work from exit tasks you will implement or have implemented?	
10. What's unique, compared to the other Formative 5 techniques, about the exit task?	

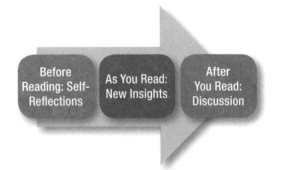

As You Read: New Insights. Use the following chart to record your notes.

Thoughts on Chapter 5: Exit Tasks					
Reading Notes	Page	I wonder ...	This connects to ...	I'd like to try ...	I am worried about ...

After You Read: Discussion. Chapter 5 introduces the exit task formative assessment technique as a performance-based task that occurs near the conclusion of a lesson or perhaps a major concept or topic within a lesson. After reading this chapter, begin your group session by sharing some of your thoughts about the reading. You may begin by revisiting the discussion questions introduced in the Before Reading section. Use the following graphic organizer to record your ideas from the group discussion, identifying particular Aha! moments from the group, and then determining next steps (Let's Try!) for individuals or the group. As the group shares, participants can record interesting thoughts, summaries, or new questions developed from the reading. As with the other chapter reviews, note that the Aha! section is a place to record new insights and the Let's Try! is the actionable item that the group will want to try after reading and discussing the chapter.

Sharing	Aha!	Let's Try!

REFERENCES

Black, P., & Wiliam, D. (1998). Assessment and classroom learning. *Assessment in Education: Principles, Policy & Practice, 5*(1), 7–74.

Black, P. J., & Wiliam, D. (2009). Developing the theory of formative assessment. *Educational Assessment, Evaluation and Accountability, 21*(1), 5–31.

Bloom, B. S. (1969). Some theoretical issues relating to educational evaluation. In H. G. Richey & R. W. Tyler (Eds.), *Educational evaluation: New roles, new means, pt. 2* (Vol. 68, pp. 26–50). Chicago: University of Chicago Press.

Darling-Hammond, L. (1994). Performance-based assessment and educational equity. *Harvard Educational Review, 64*(1), 5–31.

Fennell, F. (1998). A through the lens look at moments in classroom assessment. In G. Bright & J. M. Joyner (Eds.), *Classroom assessment in mathematics* (pp. 161–166). Lanham, MD: United Press of America.

Fennell, F. (2011). All means all. In F. Fennell (Ed.), *Achieving fluency: Special education and mathematics* (pp. 1–14). Reston, VA: National Council of Teachers of Mathematics.

Fennell, F., Kobett, B., & Wray, J. (2015). Classroom-based formative assessments: Guiding teaching and learning. In C. Suurtamm (Ed.) & A. McDuffie (Series Ed.), *Annual perspectives in mathematics education: Assessment to enhance teaching and learning* (pp. 51–62). Reston, VA: National Council of Teachers of Mathematics.

Fisher, D., & Frey, N. (2004). *Improving adolescent literacy: Strategies at work*. Upper Saddle River, NJ: Pearson Prentice Hall.

Freudenthal, H. (1973). *Mathematics as an educational task*. New York: Springer.

Ginsburg, H. P. (1997). *Entering the child's mind: The clinical interview in psychological research and practice*. New York: Cambridge University Press.

Ginsburg, H. P., & Dolan, A. O. (2011). Assessment. In F. Fennell (Ed.), *Achieving fluency: Special education and mathematics* (pp. 85–103). Reston, VA: National Council of Teachers of Mathematics.

Hiebert, J., Carpenter, T. P., Fennema, E., Fuson, K. C., Wearne, D., Hanlie, H., Olivier, A., & Human, P. (1997). *Making sense: Teaching and learning mathematics with understanding*. Portsmouth, NH: Heinemann.

Jacobs, V. R., Lamb, L. L., & Philipp, R. A. (2010). Professional noticing of children's mathematical thinking. *Journal for Research in Mathematics Education, 41*(2), 169–202.

Kahl, S. R., Hofman, P., & Bryant, S. (2013). Assessment literacy standards and performance measures for teacher candidates and practicing teachers. Retrieved from https://www.measured progress.org/caep-paper.

Larson, M. R., Fennell, F., Adams, T. L., Dixon, J. K., Kobett, B. M., & Wray, J. A. (2012). *Common core mathematics in a PLC at work: Grades 3–5.* Bloomington, IN: Solution Tree Press.

Leahy, S., Lyon, C., Thompson, M., & Wiliam, D. (2005). Classroom assessment: Minute-by-minute and day-by-day. *Educational Leadership, 63*(3), 18–24.

National Council of Teachers of Mathematics. (1991). *Professional standards for teaching mathematics.* Reston, VA: Author.

National Council of Teachers of Mathematics. (1995). *Assessment standards for school mathematics.* Reston, VA: Author.

National Council of Teachers of Mathematics. (2014). *Principles to actions: Ensuring mathematics success for all.* Reston, VA: Author.

National Governors Association Center for Best Practices & Council of Chief State School Officers. (2010). *Common core state standards for mathematics.* Washington, DC: Author.

National Mathematics Advisory Panel. (2008). *Foundations for success: The final report of the National Mathematics Advisory Panel.* Washington, DC: U.S. Department of Education.

Nelson, H. (2013). *Testing more, teaching less—What America's obsession with student testing costs in money and lost instructional time.* Washington, DC: American Federation of Teachers.

Popham, J. (2011). Formative assessment—A process and not a test. *Education Week, 30*(21), 35–37.

Scriven, M. (1967). The methodology of evaluation. In R. W. Tyler, R. M. Gagné, & M. Scriven (Eds.), *Perspectives of curriculum evaluation* (Vol. 1, pp. 39–83). Chicago: RAND.

Shavelson, R. J., Baxter, G. P., & Pine, J. (1992). Performance assessments: Political rhetoric and measurement reality. *Educational Researcher, 21*(4), 22–27.

Smith, M. S., & Stein, M. K. (1998). Selecting and creating mathematical tasks: From research to practice. *Mathematics Teaching in the Middle School, 3*(5), 344–349.

Smith, M. S., & Stein, M. K. (2011). *5 practices for orchestrating productive mathematics discussions.* Reston, VA: National Council of Teachers of Mathematics.

Spangler, D. A., Kim, J., Cross, D., Kilic, H., Iscimen, F., & Swanagan, D. (2014). Using rich tasks to promote discourse. In K. Karp (Ed.) & A. R. McDuffie (Series Ed.), *Annual perspectives in mathematics education 2014: Using research to improve instruction* (pp. 97–104). Reston, VA: National Council of Teachers of Mathematics.

Stein, M. K., Smith, M. S., Henningsen, M., & Silver, E. A. (2009). *Implementing standards-based mathematics instruction: A casebook for professional development* (2nd ed.). New York: Teachers College Press.

Stiggins, R. J. (2005). From formative assessment to assessment FOR learning: A path to success in standards-based schools. *Phi Delta Kappan, 87*(4), 324–328.

Sueltz, B. A., Boynton, H., & Sauble, I. (1946). The measurement of understandings in elementary school mathematics. In W. Brownell (Ed.), *Measurement of understanding: 45th yearbook of the National Society for the Study of Education, Part I.* Chicago: University of Chicago Press.

Understanding formative assessment: A special report. *Education Week* (2015, November 9). Retrieved from http://www.edweek.org/ew/collections/understanding-formative-assessment-special-report/.

Weaver, F. J. (1955). Big dividends from little interviews. *Arithmetic Teacher, 2*(2), 40–47.

Webb, N. (1997). *Research monograph number 6: Criteria for alignment of expectations and assessments on mathematics and science education.* Washington, DC: Council of Chief State School Officers.

Wiliam, D. (2011). *Embedded formative assessment.* Bloomington, IN: Solution Tree Press.

Wiliam, D., & Leahy, S. (2015). *Embedding formative assessment: Practical techniques for K–12 classrooms.* West Palm Beach, FL: Learning Sciences International.

Wiliam, D., & Thompson, M. (2007). Integrating assessment with instruction: What will it take to make it work? In C. A. Dwyer (Ed.), *The future of assessment: Shaping teaching and learning.* Mahwah, NJ: Lawrence Erlbaum.

Willingham, D. T. (2009). *Why don't students like school? A cognitive scientist answers questions about how the mind works and what it means for your classroom.* San Francisco: Jossey-Bass.

INDEX

CM CORWIN
MATHEMATICS

Supporting Teachers, Empowering Learners

Why Corwin Mathematics?

We've all heard this—"either you are a math person, or you are not." At Corwin Mathematics, we believe ALL students should have the opportunity to be successful in math! Trusted experts in math education such as Linda Gojak, Ruth Harbin Miles, John SanGiovanni, Skip Fennell, Gary Martin, and many more offer clear and practical guidance to help all students move from surface to deep mathematical understanding, from favoring procedural knowledge over conceptual learning, and from rote memorization to true comprehension. **We deliver research-based, high-quality content that is classroom-tested and ready to be used in your lessons**—today!

Through books, videos, consulting, and online tools, we offer a truly **blended learning experience that helps teachers demystify math for students.** The user-friendly design and format of our resources provides not only the best classroom-based professional guidance, but many activities, lesson plans, rubrics, and templates to help you implement changes at your own pace in order to sustain learning improvement over time. We are **committed to empowering every learner.** With our forward-thinking and practical offerings, Corwin Mathematics helps you enable all students to realize the power and beauty of math and its connection to everything they do.

Warm Regards,
The Corwin Mathematics Team

www.corwin.com | CALL 800-233-9936 | FAX 805-375-1711

New titles from Corwin Mathematics!

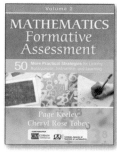
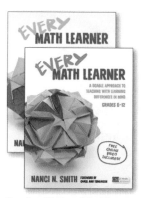

A SAGE Publishing Company

Helping educators make the greatest impact

CORWIN HAS ONE MISSION: to enhance education through intentional professional learning.

We build long-term relationships with our authors, educators, clients, and associations who partner with us to develop and continuously improve the best evidence-based practices that establish and support lifelong learning.

NATIONAL COUNCIL OF TEACHERS OF MATHEMATICS

The National Council of Teachers of Mathematics is the public voice of mathematics education, supporting teachers to ensure equitable mathematics learning of the highest quality for all students through vision, leadership, professional development, and research.